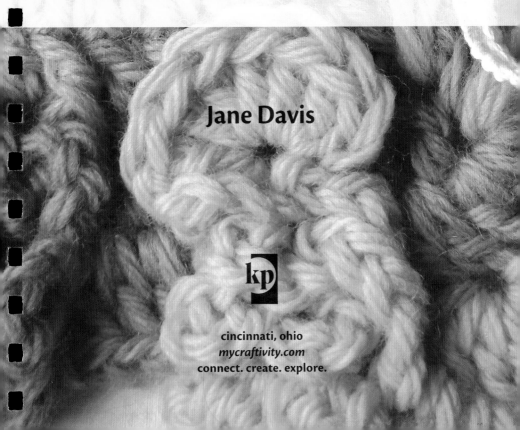

crochet

THE COMPLETE GUIDE

Jane Davis

kp

cincinnati, ohio
mycraftivity.com
connect. create. explore.

media

Other fine Krause Publications titles are available from your local bookstore, craft supply store, online retailer or visit our Web site at www.fwmedia.com.

13 12 11   5 4 3

DISTRIBUTED IN CANADA BY FRASER DIRECT
100 Armstrong Avenue
Georgetown, ON, Canada L7G 5S4
Tel: (905) 877-4411

DISTRIBUTED IN THE U.K. AND EUROPE BY DAVID & CHARLES
Brunel House, Newton Abbot, Devon, TQ12 4PU, England
Tel: (+44) 1626 323200, Fax: (+44) 1626 323319
E-mail: postmaster@davidandcharles.co.uk

DISTRIBUTED IN AUSTRALIA BY CAPRICORN LINK
P.O. Box 704, S. Windsor NSW, 2756 Australia
Tel: (02) 4577-3555

Library of Congress Cataloging in Publication Data

Davis, Jane
   Crochet : the complete guide / Jane Davis. -- 1st ed.
       p. cm.
   Includes index.
   ISBN 978-0-89689-697-0 (alk. paper)
   1. Crocheting. 2. Crocheting--Patterns. I. Title.
   TT820.D368 2009
   746.43'4041--dc22
                                2008048723

Editor: Jennifer Claydon
Cover Designer: Julie Barnett
Interior Designer: Lauren Yusko
Production coordinator: Matt Wagner
Photograpers: Jane Davis and Ric Deliantoni
Illustrator: Jane Davis
Stylist: Nora Martini
Make-up Artist: Gina Weathersby
Technical Editor: Karen Manthey

DEDICATION

For my sister Joan

ACKNOWLEDGMENTS

I have had a great time working on this book. It has been a
lot of fun trying out new stitch ideas and collecting them
together with many of the classics that I've used for years.
There have been several people who have helped me get this
book together that I would like to thank.

All the people at Krause Publications have been a joy to
work with, especially my editor Jenni Claydon. Thank you for
your deadlines, your patience and your attention to detail.

Thank you, Candy Wiza at Krause Publications, for
saying yes to this idea and for being so supportive and
understanding. Thank you also to all the people at Krause
Publications who helped to get this book out, especially Julie
Barnett, who designed the cover, and Lauren Yusko, who
designed the interior of the book.

Finally, I'd like to thank my family, Rich, Jeff, Andrew and
Jonathan, for living with my yarn that's still everywhere.

Contents

CHAPTER THREE
Basic Projects ~ 204

Introduction

Crochet is an amazing and incredibly varied needleart. It's hard to believe that from a simple hook and string you can create an unending number of patterns. The scope of crochet ranges from everyday utilitarian objects to highly ornate decorative items and expressions of art. Because of the many possibilities of crochet, the title of this book is a bit of a misnomer: How can any book about an evolving technique be complete? I have tried to include all that I can on the subject, starting with the basics. Stitch patterns follow the basics, with a wide variety of crochet techniques showcased, such as Tunisian crochet (see page 184) and bead crochet (see page 144). The book ends with several patterns for sweaters, scarves and more; you can follow the patterns I provided, or use them as jumping-off points to try out different stitches, patterns and techniques.

This book is meant for crocheters of all skill levels, both as a how-to guide, and as a reference. I hope you will come back to it again and again for ideas and information on all the different styles of crochet, for making everything from thread crochet lace, to thick, cozy afghans. I included everything here that I would want in a crochet reference book, and I know I will be checking it often to look up a pattern or check techniques. I hope that you find as much information and inspiration reading this book as I did writing it!

CHAPTER ONE

Crochet Basics

From tools to techniques, this chapter contains all the information you need to get started with crochet or to take your projects to the next level. Learn about yarns and how they impact your project. Discover the tools that will make your stitches dance. Practice crochet techniques from beginner to advanced. It's all right here!

Yarn

Fiber Content

Many different types of fiber are used to produce yarn, each with its own properties. The variety ranges from animal fibers such as wool, alpaca and mohair, to plant fibers such as cotton, hemp and linen. There is also a wide range of synthetic yarn available. Many yarns are blends of several types of fiber, each of which lends inherent characteristics to the blend and affects the feel and quality of the yarn. Following are descriptions of the most common fibers currently available.

Wool yarn can be made of fiber from any type of sheep. It is the classic crochet yarn. Wool yarns are springy, making them ideal for most types of crochet. The spring in wool yarn makes it give a little as it is worked, allowing for many different types of stitches. The yarn can be coarse or soft, depending on many factors, including the type of sheep the wool comes from, the processing of the fibers and the final treatment of the yarn.

Alpaca and llama yarns have gained in popularity over the years as a softer alternative to wool yarn. Yarn made from alpaca fiber is generally smoother and softer than wool yarn. Llama yarn is softer than wool, as well, but not as soft as alpaca. However, neither has as much spring as sheep's wool.

Mohair yarn is characterized by long fibers that create a soft halo around a tightly twisted core yarn. Mohair yarn produces a fuzzy fabric when used in crochet. To crochet mohair yarns, work with loose tension on the stitches so the fibers don't tangle.

Silk yarn adds a beautiful sheen to crocheted items. It has very little give and can be slippery to work with, but the results are often worth the trouble. Yarn made from silk noil, or silk waste, has a matte texture and has properties similar to soft cotton yarns.

Exotic yarns are increasingly common in the yarn market today. Fibers from the angora rabbit, cashmere goat, yak, buffalo, musk ox and camel are easier to find than ever. These luxurious fibers, though expensive, produce very soft yarns, making them ideal for accents, small projects and luxurious gifts.

Cotton yarn comes in a wide variety of preparations; it can be soft and fuzzy, or smooth with a soft sheen. Cotton yarn doesn't have as much spring as wool yarn, so it can be a bit more difficult to work with. It is commonly used in all sizes, from thin threads for lace, to thicker yarns for blankets and sweaters.

Linen yarn is stiffer than cotton, but it wears well when finished. It can be machine-washed and -dried. Crocheted linen fabrics can have a fluid drape or a stiff structure, depending on how tightly the stitches are formed.

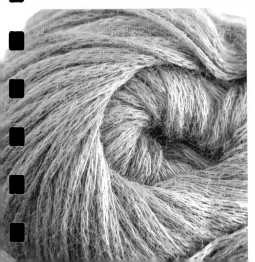

Bamboo and hemp yarns are plant-based yarns that have become available recently. Bamboo, like cotton, doesn't have as much spring as wool yarns, but it does have a lustrous sheen and softer drape than most cottons. It is easy to work with and comes in several weights. Hemp yarns are rougher than bamboo and have a natural, unfinished look.

Organic yarns have been gaining popularity lately, but this classification can be confusing. A number of yarns are made with some processes that are organic and some that are not. To be truly organic, each process used in the yarn production must be organic. Check the yarn's label for information about the yarn.

Synthetic yarns are the most widely available yarns. Acrylic, polyester and other man-made fibers fall into this category. Yarns made from these fibers attempt to mimic natural fiber qualities or have their own unique characteristics.

Blended yarns contain more than one type of fiber. Most yarns today fall into this category. Blending fibers can create wonderful yarns because the good qualities of different fibers can be emphasized, while the undesired qualities can be minimized. For example, silk added to wool increases shine and softness, and wool added to alpaca increases the spring of the finished yarn.

Texture

When choosing yarn for a project, fiber content isn't the only factor to consider. There are also many choices in yarn textures, from smooth, springy sock yarns, to airy, fluffy mohair blends, to sparkly metallic yarns. Each type of yarn texture has its own unique qualities that can affect the crocheting process as well as how a project looks and feels when it is finished. Following are descriptions of many of the types of yarn textures available today.

Eyelash yarn is composed of a core strand with fringe-like strands of fiber. Worked by itself, or held along with another yarn, eyelash yarn creates a soft, furry fabric. It is easiest to work this yarn with a larger size hook than you normally would use for a smooth yarn of comparable weight, since the stray strands can get caught in the stitches as you work them.

Chenille yarn is a soft, fuzzy yarn that has a texture similar to velour fabric. It is made of a thin, tightly twisted core with short fibers radiating out perpendicular to the core, creating a round, soft yarn. Most chenille yarns are made from cotton, silk or synthetic fibers. It can be difficult to crochet with this type of yarn, as it has no springiness, or give, and tends to create uneven stitches. This can sometimes be corrected if you dampen the finished item and put it in the dryer. Make a large swatch with chenille yarn before beginning a project to see how the yarn and stitches interact.

Metallic yarn is made from natural or synthetic fibers combined with metal or with a material that looks like metal, such as mylar. These yarns can often be stiff or scratchy, so they work best as accents or in projects that won't be worn next to the skin.

Ribbon yarn, also known as tape yarn, is a flat yarn that varies in width from ⅛"-½" (3mm-13mm) and sometimes more. Any ribbon can be used as yarn, but ribbon yarns are made soft for easy knitting. Ribbon or tape yarns are usually made from cotton, silk, wool blends or synthetics. You can make a ruffle with loosely woven ribbon or tape yarns by crocheting tightly into the edge of the yarn with a thin yarn, gathering the tape as you work.

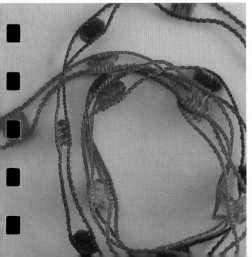

Railroad yarn resembles railroad tracks or a ladder. It is composed of two thin, parallel cords attached at regular intervals by horizontal bars of thread. Most railroad yarns are made from synthetic fibers. Railroad yarn is flat and usually no thicker than ¼" (6mm) wide.

Spaced accent yarn has a thin core with accents such as sequins or tufts of yarn spaced at regular intervals throughout the yarn. These yarns are generally carried along with another yarn so the core strand is inconspicuous and the accents highlight the project.

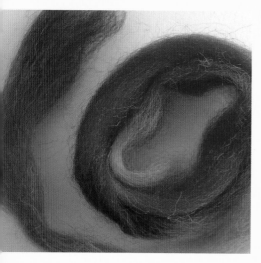

Roving is wool that has not yet been spun, but it can be used in crochet instead of yarn. Roving is soft and thick and pulls apart easily, so it must be handled with care. To crochet with roving, split it into thin strips. When you reach the end of a strip, overlap the end of an old strip and a new strip and continue working with both held together. Pencil roving is roving that is about as thick as a pencil and can be crocheted without being split.

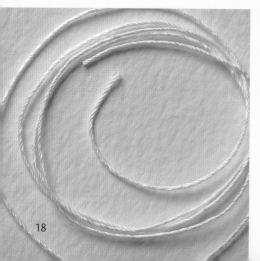

Thread can be used in crochet to create open fabrics and lace. Thread crochet is worked using smaller hooks and thin cord or thread made with cotton or synthetic fibers. All of the techniques used for crocheting with yarn can also be used for crocheting with thread, and vice versa.

Thick-and-thin yarn, also sometimes referred to as homespun yarn, varies in thickness along the length of the yarn. This can be a minor variation or a large change from very thick to very thin sections of yarn. Thick-and-thin yarns are usually wool or wool blend yarns.

Mixing Yarns

Any of the yarns described in this section can be used together to create a beautiful combination of textures. A metallic or eyelash yarn can be worked together with a plain yarn, such as homespun wool, to create a unique texture. While some yarns are manufactured from multiple strands with different textures, if you can't find exactly what you want you can choose different yarns and hold them together as one while crocheting to create your own combinations.

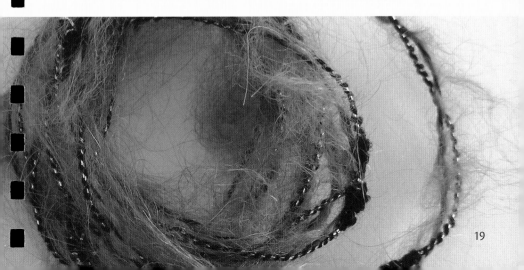

Color

The final, and some say most important, choice is the color of the yarn. Crocheters today don't just get to choose between different hues. There are also many different methods of coloring, from machine-dyed solids to one-of-a-kind hand-painted skeins. The color and the process used to color your yarn will affect your finished project. Following are many of the choices currently available.

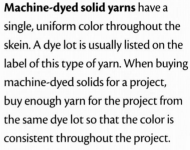

Machine-dyed solid yarns have a single, uniform color throughout the skein. A dye lot is usually listed on the label of this type of yarn. When buying machine-dyed solids for a project, buy enough yarn for the project from the same dye lot so that the color is consistent throughout the project.

Hand-dyed solid yarns are dyed with one dye color, but because they are dyed in small groups by hand, the color of the yarn varies slightly throughout each skein. This creates a subtle mottled effect in crocheted fabrics. Hand-dyed solid yarns sometimes have dye lot numbers and sometimes not, depending on the dyer's practices.

Machine-dyed variegated yarn has color changes throughout the skein of yarn. The color sequence repeats at regular intervals, usually about every yard (meter). There are also machine-dyed yarns that mimic the mottled effect of hand-dyed yarns. The color variations in machine-dyed yarns are more regular than those in hand-dyed yarns.

Hand-painted yarn is painted by a dye artist. Each skein has its own unique color sequence. Dye lots can be used for batches of yarn dyed in the same session, though each skein may have varying amounts of the different colors.

Spot-dyed yarn is hand-painted with random spots of color added to the dye scheme. The spots of color may or may not show up through the entire skein in a regular repeat.

Rainbow-dyed yarn is a variegated yarn that gradually travels through a color spectrum. This spectrum could be the whole rainbow, or could be a color progression between two colors, such as green and blue. Fabric crocheted from this type of yarn gradually changes from one color to the next.

Crochet Tools

Very few tools are needed for crochet. There are, of course, numerous gizmos and gadgets that can make crochet easier, but these basics will get you through every project.

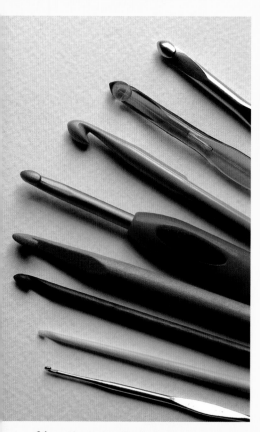

Crochet hooks are short sticks with a hook at one end for pulling yarn or thread. They can be made from wood, metal, plastic or even glass and other exotic materials. Most crochet hooks are basic and plain, but they can also be made with decorative elements and elaborate handles. Crochet hooks are usually about 5"-6" (13cm-15cm) long with a flattened area about 1½" (4cm) from the hook-end where you hold the tool between your thumb and fingers.

Anatomy of a Crochet Hook

1. Hook

Also called the tip or the head, this end of the crochet hook is used to move the yarn.

1

2

2. Throat

This section of the crochet hook widens from the hook to the full diameter of the shaft. The shape of this section varies from different manufacturers.

3

3. Shaft

The shaft is the section of the crochet hook where the stitches are held. The size of this portion of the crochet hook dictates the size of the stitches.

4

Unfortunately, hook sizes are not standardized throughout the industry, so sizes may vary from brand to brand. Checking the metric diameter of the shaft is the only way to be sure of what size hook you have. Choosing the hook that results in the correct gauge for a pattern is the most important criterion for working a project to the finished size indicated, so try different sized hooks until your swatch has the project gauge listed, not necessarily the same size hook listed in the instructions. A guide to crochet hook sizes can be found on page 248.

5

4. Thumb grip

This flattened section is where the hook is held between the thumb and fingers. Some crochet hooks are shaped in this area to help you hold the hook more comfortably.

5. Handle

The remainder of the hook is gripped with the fingers not resting on the thumb grip.

Graph paper and pencils come in handy when altering the size or shape of a pattern, or when charting a design of your own.

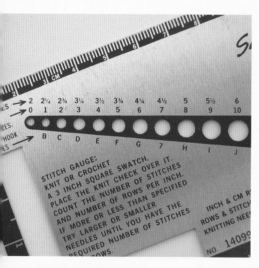

A hook gauge has labeled holes of different diameters that can be used to measure a crochet hook. The smallest hole your hook will slide into is the size of your hook.

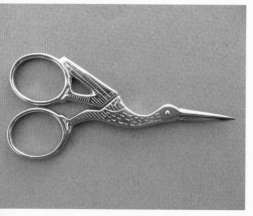

Scissors are useful to have on hand for snipping yarn ends while working on a crochet project.

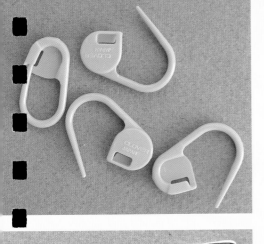

Stitch markers are small, open rings that slide into the stitches you want to note, such as those at the beginning of the round in circular crochet, or those with a change in the pattern.

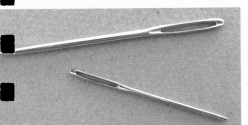

Tapestry needles are blunt needles with large eyes used for weaving in the ends of yarn. Sewing needles can be used for adding beads to yarn or sewing details onto the finished crochetwork.

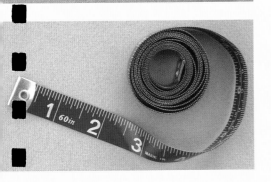

A tape measure is used throughout the crochet process to measure your gauge and your progress and to help when blocking your finished piece.

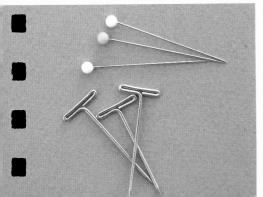

Straight pins and T-pins are used to hold your finished item in place when you block your pieces to shape.

Crochet Terms

There are only a few special terms you need to know to master crochet, but they are important. Learn these words and concepts in advance and they'll serve you well.

Gauge is a measurement of the number of stitches across 4" (10cm) of crocheted fabric and the number of rows over 4" (10cm) of crocheted fabric. It is the basis of pattern instructions for garment sizing and is critical in creating a project that matches the size indicated in the instructions. It is very important to work up a test swatch for your project that matches the gauge indicated on the pattern.

Start with the hook size and yarn weight indicated by your pattern. You can learn more about hook size on pages 25 and 248. The yarn weight will be indicated on the label that came with the yarn. For a chart of standard yarn weights, see page 247. If your gauge with the pattern's recommended yarn weight and hook size matches the pattern, you can proceed with the project.

If your gauge does not match the pattern, you can adjust your gauge by working with a larger or smaller hook, or changing the yarn you are using. You will need to make a new test swatch for each trial, but it is well worth the effort to create a garment that matches the size you wish to make.

Pattern instructions can be provided in several different formats. They can be written out as text, displayed on a chart, shown using symbols, or any combination of these.

Text instructions can be written in complete sentences or written using abbreviations. There are some abbreviations that are commonly used by most designers, and some that are unique to each designer. A list of the abbreviations used in this book can be found in the Glossary on page 245.

Charts are used when a grid pattern is being worked, such as filet crochet, single crochet colorwork or bead crochet. Because all the stitches are uniform, you only need to know where to fill in an area of netting in filet crochet, use a different color in colorwork crochet or where to add a bead in bead crochet. Any stitches that vary from the standard stitches are explained in a key.

Some crochet patterns use symbols as a representation of a pattern, showing roughly how the design will look when finished. The symbols can sometimes show every detail of what needs to be done to complete the design, or sometimes may need further explanation in some key areas of the design. When there is a repeated design, often only a single portion of the pattern is shown. A key of the symbols used in this book can be found in the Glossary on page 246.

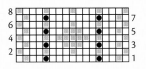

Basic Crochet Techniques

Crochet starts with basic techniques; many more details and complexities will reveal themselves as you learn. This section starts out with the most basic steps. Once you understand the first concepts you can progress to the many other possibilities crochet has to offer. As you begin, remember that most things are more difficult at the beginning and become easier as you practice. Practice these steps and you will be crocheting in no time!

Attention Left-Handers!

The instructions in this book are written from a right-handed point of view. If you are left-handed, you can learn to crochet as shown here, or reverse the directions for holding the hook in your left hand.

Holding the Hook

There are two common ways to hold a crochet hook. Either position illustrated below can be used, or any other way that is comfortable. You may have people tell you that one way is better than the other, but in the end it's which way you are most comfortable holding the hook that is the right way for you.

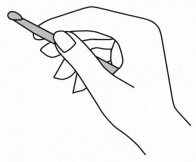

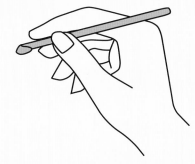

You can hold the hook with the handle below your hand, the same way you hold a knife.

Or, you can hold the hook with the handle above your hand, the same way you are taught to hold a pencil in school.

Holding the Yarn

When crocheting you need to have control over both the hook and the yarn you are working with. The yarn is wrapped around the index finger of your left hand, and your right hand moves the hook over and under the yarn to create the stitches. You also use your left hand to hold the fabric you have already crocheted, to keep an even tension on the yarn so the stitches will be even.

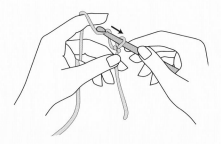

Making a Slip Knot •

Most crochet projects start with a slip knot. This is the process of creating an adjustable loop that you tighten onto your crochet hook.

1 Make loop
Hold the end of the yarn in your left hand, then use your right hand to make a loop of yarn about 6" (15cm) away from the end of the yarn. Pass the top strand of yarn under the loop, then pull a new loop up through the first loop.

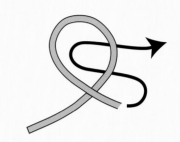

2 Insert hook
Slide the hook through the new loop of yarn.

3 Tighten knot
Pull on the yarn ends to snug the slip knot on the shaft of the crochet hook. The slip knot should not be tight.

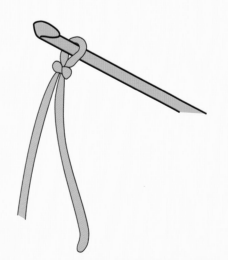

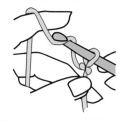

Yarn Over, or Wrapping the Yarn around the Hook

Every stitch in crochet involves wrapping the yarn around the hook, also known as a yarn over, often several times. The yarn is always wrapped around the hook the same way. Bring the yarn up from behind and over the hook from right to left.

Making a Chain (ch) ⌒

A chain is the beginning foundation for almost all crochet projects. It is also used at the beginning of rows and throughout many patterns in crochet.

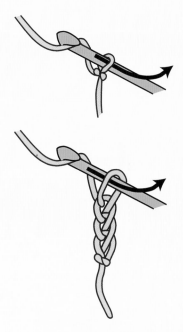

1 **First stitch**
Make a slip knot and place it on the crochet hook. Loop the working yarn around the hook and slide the hook through the slip knot, pulling the wrapped yarn through the slip knot. This will create a new loop on the hook. Gently pull on the working yarn to make the new loop about the same size as the slip knot.

2 **Continue chain**
Repeat Step 1 for each chain stitch required by your pattern. Make each loop the same size as the previous loops.

Creating Even Stitches

The size of the stitches you make is determined partly by the size of the crochet hook you use and partly by how tight you pull the yarn as each stitch is made. The shaft of the hook sets the gauge of your loops, and this is where you should work your stitches (see *Anatomy of a Crochet Hook*, page 25). It is important not to work your stitches on the throat of the crochet hook; if you do, you will have trouble getting your loop off the hook. If you pull your stitches too tight on the shaft, you will also have a hard time moving them off of the hook. For even tension, pull the yarn until it fits snugly around the thickest part of the crochet hook's shaft. This will create uniform stitches that are loose enough to slide off of the hook.

The bottom rows of stitches in this swatch were worked with even tension and the top rows of stitches were not.

The Parts of a Chain

A chain is composed of a yarn tail, a slip knot, chain stitches, the loop of yarn on the hook, the yarn wrapped around the hook and the working end of the yarn. Each stitch in a foundation chain has three parts: the front loop, the back loop and the back bump of the chain. When you work the first row of stitches on the foundation chain, you can insert the hook into any one of these parts to make your stitch.

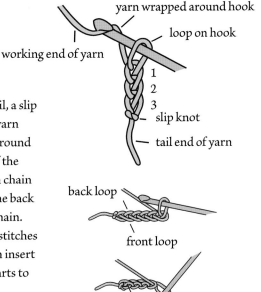

yarn wrapped around hook

loop on hook

working end of yarn

1
2
3
— slip knot

— tail end of yarn

back loop

front loop

back bump

Single Crochet (sc) × +

Single crochet is one of the most basic stitches in crochet and it is used in many different stitch patterns. Single crochet stitches can be worked into a foundation chain or into stitches from a previous row.

1 Begin stitch

To work a single crochet, begin by inserting the hook into the chain or stitch indicated by the pattern. If you are stitching into a foundation chain, you can insert the hook into the front loop, the back loop or the back bump of the chain to make your stitch. The lower right illustration shows the hook working into the back loop. If you are working in a stitch from a previous row, always insert the hook under the top 2 loops of the stitch as shown in the above right illustration, unless the instructions indicate otherwise.

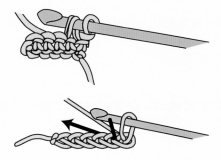

2 Continue stitch

Wrap the yarn around the hook and pull it through the loop closest to the hook. After you pull the wrapped yarn through, 2 loops will remain on the hook.

3 Finish stitch

Wrap the yarn around the hook again and pull it through both loops on the hook. There will be 1 loop on the hook.

Creating Single Crochet Fabric

Now you know everything you need to know to start crocheting. Let's put all the pieces together to create a piece of crocheted fabric.

1 **Create foundation**
Choose a yarn to work with. Refer to the ballband on the yarn to choose an appropriately sized crochet hook. Make a slip knot (see *Making a Slip Knot*, page 32). Chain 6 stitches (see *Making a Chain*, page 33). Skip the chain stitch next to the hook and work a single crochet into the next chain (see *Single Crochet*, page 35).

2 **Finish first row**
Work single crochets into the next 4 chain stitches—5 single crochet stitches total. To work the next row, turn the crocheting so that the back side of the crocheting is facing you.

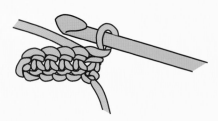

3 Begin next row

Chain 1, then insert the hook into the top 2 loops of the first stitch from the previous row.

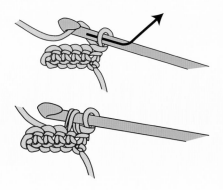

4 Complete first stitch

Work a single crochet to form the first stitch of the new row.

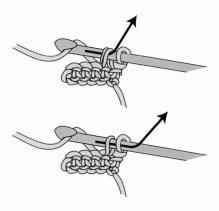

5 Finish second row

Work a single crochet in each stitch across the row. Repeat Steps 3–5 until the fabric is as long as you desire. Secure the last stitch (see *Securing the Last Stitch*, page 39).

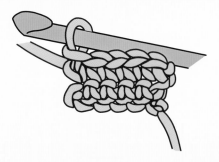

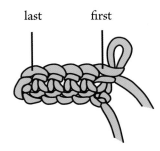

last   first

*In this sample, the chains
do not count as stitches,
resulting in a wavy edge.*

first

last

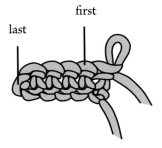

*In this sample, the
chains do count as
stitches, resulting in
a smoother edge.*

Beginning and Ending a Row

When working a row of crochet, sometimes the chain stitches at the beginning
of the row count as one of the stitches of the row, and sometimes they don't. The
pattern you are working with will indicate whether or not the chains count as
stitches. If the chain doesn't count as a stitch, work into every stitch from the
previous row. This method creates a slightly wavy edge. If the first chain counts
as a stitch, then skip the first stitch and work into all the other stitches of the
row. On the next row, work into the chain at the end of the row as if it were a
stitch. This method creates a smoother edge. Directions differ from designer to
designer and project to project, but in this book, unless it is otherwise specified,
the chain at the beginning of the row is not counted as a stitch.

Securing the Last Stitch

When you have finished crocheting, you need to secure the last loop of the last stitch to complete the piece. This will keep your work from unraveling.

1 **Secure stitch**
Cut the yarn leaving a 6" (15cm) tail. Pull the tail through the last loop using the hook. Pull the tail until the last loop tightens securely around the yarn tail.

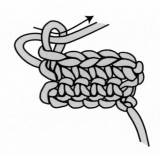

Weaving in Ends

Weaving in the yarn ends on crocheted fabric provides a neat appearance for your finished piece.

1 **Weave in end**
Thread a yarn end on a tapestry needle. Pass the needle back through stitches close to the yarn end for about 1" (3cm) in one direction, then back the other way so that the yarn is buried in the stitches and is anchored in place by passing back over itself. Try to pierce the yarn when you pass back in the opposite direction. Cut the yarn close to the stitches and stretch the crocheted fabric a little so that the thread end disappears into the fabric.

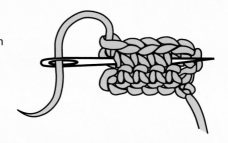

Beyond Basic Techniques

Beyond the basic techniques, there is so much more to crochet. The following techniques can be used to create the wonderful textures, patterns and colors that make crocheting such a rich and varied needleart.

Slip Stitch (sl st) ●

A slip stitch is the smallest stitch in crochet. It is used to attach sections of stitches together, or to discreetly move the beginning of the thread to a new location in preparation for a new row or round of stitches.

1 **Begin stitch**
Insert the crochet hook into the chain or stitch indicated by the crochet pattern.

2 **Finish stitch**
Wrap the yarn around the hook and pull through the chain and the loop on the hook. You will have one loop on the hook.

Half Double Crochet (hdc)

A half double crochet stitch is the next step beyond a single crochet stitch. It is taller than a single crochet stitch.

1 **Begin stitch**
Wrap the yarn around the hook once. Insert the crochet hook into the chain or stitch indicated by your pattern. When beginning a row with a half double crochet, you will usually start by chaining 2 and working into the third chain from the hook.

2 **Continue stitch**
Wrap the yarn around the hook and pull it through the loop closest to the hook. After you pull the wrapped yarn through, 3 loops will remain on the hook.

3 **Finish stitch**
Wrap the yarn around the hook again and pull it through the remaining loops on the hook. There will be 1 loop on the hook.

Double Crochet (dc) ⊤

Double crochet is the most commonly used stitch in crochet. It is taller than single crochet or half double crochet and is quicker to accomplish than triple crochet. Because of these factors it is about the fastest stitch to work in crochet and has an easy rhythm, both of which make it a popular stitch.

1 Begin stitch

Wrap the yarn around the hook once. Insert the crochet hook into the chain or stitch indicated by your pattern. When beginning a row with a double crochet, you will usually start by chaining 3 and working into the fourth chain from the hook.

2 Continue stitch

Wrap the yarn around the hook and pull it through the loop closest to the hook. After you pull the wrapped yarn through, 3 loops will remain on the hook.

3 Continue stitch

Wrap the yarn around the hook and pull it through the 2 loops closest to the hook. After you pull the wrapped yarn through, 2 loops will remain on the hook.

4 Finish stitch

Wrap the yarn around the hook again and pull it through the remaining loops on the hook. There will be 1 loop on the hook.

Half Triple Crochet (htr)

A half triple crochet isn't an official stitch. I use it sometimes as a transition from double crochet to triple crochet, but it is not something you will run across in other books, magazines or instructions.

1 Begin stitch
Wrap the yarn around the hook twice. Insert the crochet hook into the chain or stitch indicated by your pattern. When beginning a row with a half triple crochet, you will usually start by chaining 3 and working into the fifth chain from the hook.

2 Continue stitch
Wrap the yarn around the hook and pull it through the loop closest to the hook. After you pull the wrapped yarn through, 4 loops will remain on the hook.

3 Continue stitch
Wrap the yarn around the hook and pull it through the 2 loops closest to the hook. After you pull the wrapped yarn through, 3 loops will remain on the hook.

4 Finish stitch
Wrap the yarn around the hook again and pull it through the remaining loops on the hook. There will be 1 loop on the hook.

Triple Crochet (tr)

This tall stitch adds height to a row, making it a great stitch when progressing from low to high sections in your work.

1 Begin stitch

Wrap the yarn around the hook twice. Insert the crochet hook into the chain or stitch indicated by your pattern. When beginning a row with a triple crochet, you will usually start by chaining 3 and working into the fifth chain from the hook.

2 Continue stitch

Wrap the yarn around the hook and pull it through the loop closest to the hook. After you pull the wrapped yarn through, 4 loops will remain on the hook.

3 Continue stitch

Wrap the yarn around the hook and pull it through the 2 loops closest to the hook. After you pull the wrapped yarn through, 3 loops will remain on the hook.

4 Continue stitch

Wrap the yarn around the hook and pull it through the 2 loops closest to the hook. After you pull the wrapped yarn through, 2 loops will remain on the hook.

5 Finish stitch

Wrap the yarn around the hook again and pull it through the remaining loops on the hook. There will be 1 loop on the hook.

Beyond Triple Crochet

As you can see from the progression from single crochet to double crochet to triple crochet, you can make taller stitches by wrapping the yarn around your hook additional times before beginning a stitch, then repeating the steps of making a yarn over and pulling through two loops on the hook, until you are down to just one loop. You can create stitches that are longer than triple crochet, if you need them. A double triple crochet (dtr) is the next stitch beyond triple crochet. For that stitch, you wrap the yarn around the hook three times, then work the loops off the hook two at a time. The symbols for these stitches add an additional horizontal line through the vertical bar to show how many wraps start the stitch.

Here, the yarn was wrapped five times around the hook before beginning the stitch. There are no historic names for stitches larger than a double triple crochet, but they are sometimes used in projects and designers will give the stitches names, so the names can vary from pattern to pattern.

Increases

Increasing in crochet is accomplished either by simply working more than one stitch in the same place, or by working more stitches in a single row than the previous row, such as in shells and fans.

Shells and Fans

Shells and fans are made by working two or more stitches in the same location. They can be small or very large.

Decreases

To decrease in crochet, either skip stitches from the previous row as you work the current row, or work a pattern stitch that decreases the number of stitches from the previous row, such as in clusters.

Clusters and Bobbles

With clusters and bobbles, you make each stitch into the same location, working each one to the last yarn over, keeping the last two loops of each stitch on the hook. Then with the last yarn over, you pull the hook through all the loops on the hook, gathering the stitches together at the top.

Ripples and Waves

A ripple or a wave pattern is made by working rows that include both clusters and shells or fans. The shells or fans create peaks while the clusters create troughs, making the row look like a wave.

Popcorns

Popcorns are made by working five or more double crochets in the same location, then gathering those stitches together. To gather the stitches, remove the hook and reinsert it into the top of the first and last stitch of the popcorn. Wrap the yarn around the hook, then pull the yarn through both stitches. To help the popcorn stay together at the top, you can make another yarn over and pull through the hook. However, this will create an extra chain stitch, so be sure not to work that extra stitch on the following row.

Stretched Stitches

Stretched stitches are made by inserting the hook more than one row below the current row so that, as the stitch is completed, a long strand of yarn is caught in the crocheted fabric.

Post Stitches

Post stitches are stitches that are worked in the post of a stitch (the vertical part of the stitch), rather than the top loops of the stitch. Post stitches can be worked from the front of the work (FP) or from the back of the work (BP). This technique is used to make cable patterns and other three-dimensional effects.

Bullions

Bullions are made by wrapping the yarn around the shank of the hook many times, then pulling through all the loops at once. To make a bullion the same height as the surrounding stitches, wrap the yarn around the shank of the hook until the wraps are the height of the surrounding stitches. To make the bullion into a loop, such as a flower petal, wrap the yarn around the shank of the hook until the wraps are twice the height of the surrounding stitches.

Cord and Tape

Cords can be made in several ways. The finished cord can be used as is, or braided or woven into a variety of forms. A cord can be as simple as a row of chain stitches, or more complex, such as a tube of seven or eight single crochet stitches worked in a circle. A flat cord, also known as a tape, can be made from one row of single crochet. Slip stitch cord is commonly used for bead crochet.

Reverse Crochet Edging

A finishing option is to work single crochet backwards across the edge of a piece. Working the stitches from left to right, instead of right to left, creates an undulating edge of stitches that neatly finishes the edge of the work. The trick to making this stitch is to make the stitches loose so they are the same tension as the rest of the piece.

Bead Crochet

Bead crochet incorporates beads into stitches as you work them. The beads are strung on yarn before crocheting begins, and then slid down the yarn into the work. Depending on when and how you slide the bead into a stitch, the bead can lie on the front or the back of the finished work, and can sit horizontally, vertically or diagonally. For the patterns in this book, the bead is slid to the hook before beginning the stitch, then caught in the stitch as it is made. With this method, the bead sits on the back side of the work.

Color Patterns from Row Changes

Simply changing the color of the yarn you are using from row to row can create color patterns. The color pattern depends on the structure of the stitches used. Post stitches and stretched stitches pull the color down to previous rows and patterns that use shells or combine tall and short stitches can create dramatic patterns.

Colorwork

Colorwork crochet, also known as tapestry crochet, is usually worked in single crochet, though it can also be worked using other stitches. To work colorwork crochet, two or more colors of yarn are alternately used across the row to create a design. The trick to making a smooth transition from one color to the next is to pull the new color through for the last yarn over on the stitch before the color change.

Finishing Techniques

When you have finished crocheting your project, you will need to add finishing touches to complete the piece. Following are some of the basics necessary to complete a crochet project.

Assembly

Some crochet projects can be created all as one piece, but for projects created in multiple pieces, assembly will be required.

Mattress Stitch

Mattress stitch is a firm stitch that joins the edges of two pieces of crochetwork together, such as the side seams of a sweater. To mattress stitch, take a stitch along the edge of one piece then take a stitch in the same place on the other piece. Now take another stitch in the first piece, inserting the needle where the last stitch ended. Repeat this along the length of the crocheted fabric, pulling the stitches together after several stitches have been made. The trick is to pull the stitches tight enough to hold the two pieces together, but not so tight that you gather the fabric, making it bunch up along the join.

Single Crochet Seam

Single crochet worked along the edges of two pieces of crochetwork creates a strong join between the pieces and can add a decorative element if worked on the right side of the work. To attach two pieces of crochet together with single crochet, hold the pieces together (right sides together if you want the single crochet to show on the back of the work, and wrong sides together if you want the stitches to show on the front of the work). Then work a row of single crochet along the edge, inserting the hook into the edges of both pieces at the beginning of each stitch.

Washing

After a piece is crocheted, wash it to remove dirt and oils that the yarn may have picked up during the crochet process. Follow the washing instructions from the yarn's label. Most yarns can be washed in warm (not hot) water with a gentle detergent. Do not agitate the piece too much; you want to avoid fulling, felting or stretching the piece. Unless the yarn is listed as machine washable, you may need to block the item after washing.

Felting

Felting, or fulling, is the process of taking an item made of wool and agitating it in warm soapy water until it transforms into a dense fuzzy fabric. Crocheted bags and hats are great projects to try with this technique.

Blocking

Blocking is used to shape a project and give it a more refined look. To block a piece of crochet, begin by dampening it with water or steam. Lay the piece out on a flat surface and pin it to the desired measurements, then let it dry completely. Different types of projects have different needs when it comes to blocking. Some, such as fine lace crochet, require that the fabric be stretched a great deal with details, such as points along the edges, defined by the pins that hold them in place while they dry. Others, like sweaters worked in worsted weight yarn, are generally adjusted just a bit from their original state to correct any unevenness.

Types of Crochet

Crochet can be divided into two basic categories: yarn crochet and thread crochet. Yarn crochet requires yarn and larger hooks to make blankets, sweaters and baby items, while thread crochet requires small steel hooks and fine cord or thread to make delicate items such as doilies or fine lace. Most patterns can be worked with either technique, though there are some stitch patterns that are commonly tied to one technique. Following are some of the types of crochet within the two main categories.

Filet Crochet

Filet crochet is traditionally worked with thread, though it can be worked with yarn as well. A square net is formed by a combination of double crochet and chain stitches creating an open grid. By filling in some of the spaces of the grid with double crochet as you work, you can create a pattern. A chart for filet crochet can be created with traditional symbols, but designers commonly use a square grid to chart a filet design.

Irish crochet is a lace style of thread crochet that is characterized by a combination of dense, usually floral, motifs, attached together by fine crochet netting, often filled with delicate picots throughout. The motifs are often worked over a foundation cord to create a raised design.

Freeform crochet is a technique that uses stitches in an unstructured pattern. Its focus is the color and texture of the design, rather than working rows back and forth. In this method of working you can begin with several motifs and add partial rows of stitches to them, then add other decorative stitches in any pattern or location you choose on your growing design.

Tunisian crochet is a technique in which you use a long crochet hook with a knob at the end, like a knitting needle. You pick up all the stitches in the row, working right to left, then you work the stitches off the hook one by one, working left to right to complete the row.

Tips for Success

As with any of the needlearts, there are tricks of the trade that can help make your projects move along more smoothly or help you to create a more professional-looking finished item. Here are some common tips that many crocheters use as they work on their projects.

— One of the most common complaints about crochet is that it's so easy to end up with more or fewer stitches in a row than you are supposed to have. Be sure to pay attention to the beginning and ending stitches, so that you aren't putting too many or too few stitches in the row at those places. Also, if you don't want to have to adjust the number of stitches if you get it wrong, be sure to count the number of stitches in the row after working it, so you are sure you are on track with the pattern.

— When making a garment for yourself, check the measurements against a similar item that has a fit you like and adjust the pattern to fit those measurements by lengthening or shortening the sleeve or body.

— To make sure that your sewn-in tails stay put, try to pass back over the same tail thread, piercing it so it stays in place.

CHAPTER TWO

Stitch Patterns

From basic, solid surfaces to complicated three-dimensional textures, crochet patterns are a treasure trove of design possibilities. This section covers a broad range of stitch patterns, touching on the many different forms that crochet offers, from crocheting with yarn to thread crochet, from basics and classics to new and unusual designs.

Basic Stitches and Stitch Combinations

1 Slip Stitch

Reversible

Any number of stitches

Foundation: Ch any number of sts, turn.

ROW 1: Ch 1, sl st in 2nd ch from hk and ea ch across, turn.

ROW 2: Ch 1, sl st in ea st across, turn.

Rep Row 2 to cont patt.

2 Single Crochet

Reversible

Any number of stitches

Foundation: Ch any number of sts, turn.

ROW 1: Ch 1, sc in 2nd ch from hk and ea ch across, turn.

ROW 2: Ch 1, sc in ea st across, turn.

Rep Row 2 to cont patt.

3 Half Double Crochet

Reversible

Any number of stitches

Foundation: Ch any number of sts, turn.

ROW 1: Ch 2, hdc in 3rd ch from hk and ea ch across, turn.

ROW 2: Ch 2, hdc in ea st across, turn.

Rep Row 2 to cont patt.

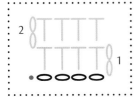

4 Double Crochet

Reversible

Any number of stitches

Foundation: Ch any number of sts, turn.

ROW 1: Ch 3, dc in 4th ch from hk and ea ch across, turn.

ROW 2: Ch 3, dc in ea st across, turn.

Rep Row 2 to cont patt.

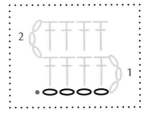

5 Half Triple Crochet

Reversible

Any number of stitches

Foundation: Ch any number of sts, turn.

ROW 1: Ch 3, htr in 4th ch from hk and ea ch across, turn.

ROW 2: Ch 3, htr in ea st across, turn.

Rep Row 2 to cont patt.

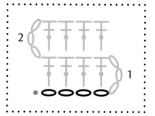

6 Triple Crochet

Reversible

Any number of stitches

Foundation: Ch any number of sts, turn.

ROW 1: Ch 4, tr in 5th ch from hk and ea ch across, turn.

ROW 2: Ch 4, tr in ea st across, turn.

Rep Row 2 to cont patt.

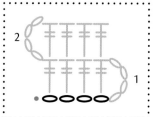

7 Alternating Rows of Single & Double Crochet

Any number of stitches

Foundation: Ch any number of sts, turn.

ROW 1: Ch 1, sc in 2nd ch from hk and ea ch across, turn.

ROW 2: Ch 2, dc in ea st across, turn.

ROW 3: Ch 1, sc in ea st across, turn.

Rep Rows 2–3 to cont patt.

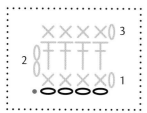

8 Graduated Crochet

Any number of stitches

Foundation: Ch any number of sts, turn.

ROW 1: Ch 1, sc in 2nd ch from hk and ea ch across, turn.

ROW 2: Ch 2, hdc in ea st across, turn.

ROW 3: Ch 3, dc in ea st across, turn.

ROW 4: Ch 4, tr in ea st across, turn.

ROW 5: Ch 1, sc in ea st across, turn.

Rep Rows 2–5 to cont patt.

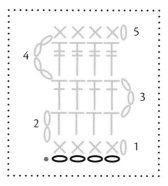

9 Waves of Single Through Triple Crochet

Reversible

Multiple of 16 stitches

Foundation: Ch a multiple of 16 sts, turn.

ROW 1: Ch 1, sc in 2nd ch from hk, sc, *2 hdc, 2 dc, 4 tr, 2 dc, 2 hdc, 4 sc; rep from * across, ending with 2 sc instead of 4 sc, turn.

ROW 2: Ch 4, *2 tr, 2 dc, 2 hdc, 4 sc, 2 hdc, 2 dc, 2 tr; rep from * across, turn.

ROW 3: Ch 1, *2 sc, 2 hdc, 2 dc, 4 tr, 2 dc, 2 hdc, 2 sc; rep from * across, turn.

Rep Rows 2–3 to cont patt.

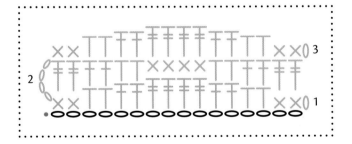

10 Pebble Stitch

Reversible

Multiple of 2 stitches

Foundation: Ch a multiple of 2 sts, turn.

ROW 1: Ch 1, sc in 2nd ch from hk, *dc, sc; rep from * to last ch, dc, turn.

ROW 2: Ch 1, *sc in dc, dc in sc; rep from * across, turn.

Rep Row 2 to cont patt.

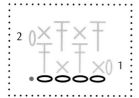

11 Wedges

Reversible

Multiple of 4 stitches

Foundation: Ch a multiple of 4 sts, turn.

ROW 1: Ch 1, sc in 2nd ch from hk, sc, 2 dc, *2 sc, 2 dc; rep from * across, turn.

ROW 2: Ch 1, *2 sc, 2 dc; rep from * across, turn.

Rep Row 2 to cont patt.

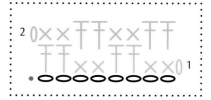

12 Single Crochet, Chain One

Reversible

Any even number of stitches

Foundation: Ch any even number of sts, turn.

ROW 1: Ch 2, sc in 4th ch from hk, *ch 1, sk 1, sc in next ch; rep from * across, turn.

ROW 2: Ch 2, sc in ch-1 space, *ch 1, sc in next ch-1 space; rep from * across, making last sc in ch sp at end of row, turn.

Rep Row 2 to cont patt.

13 Double Crochet, Chain One

Reversible

Any even number of stitches

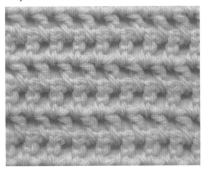

Foundation: Ch any even number of sts, turn.

ROW 1: Ch 4, dc in 6th ch from hk, *ch 1, sk 1, dc in next ch; rep from * across, turn.

ROW 2: Ch 4, dc in ch-1 space, *ch 1, dc in next ch-1 space; rep from * across, making last sc in ch sp at end of row, turn.

Rep Row 2 to cont patt.

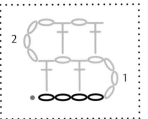

14 Basic Filet Crochet

Multiple of 12 stitches, plus 1

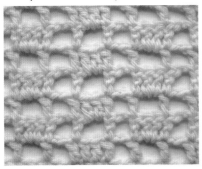

Foundation: Ch a multiple of 12 sts, plus 1, turn.

ROW 1: Ch 3, dc in 4th ch from hk, *3 dc, (ch 2, sk 2, dc in next ch) 3 times; rep from * across, turn.

ROW 2: Ch 5, sk ch sp, dc in next dc, 2 dc in ch-2 sp, dc in next dc, *ch 2, sk ch sp, dc in next dc, ch 2, sk 2 dc, dc in next dc, ch 2, sk ch sp, dc in next dc, 2 dc in ch-2 sp, dc in next dc; rep from * to last 2 squares, ch 2, sk ch sp, dc in dc, ch 2, sk 2 dc, dc in dc, turn.

ROW 3: Ch 3, dc in dc, *2 dc in ch sp, dc in dc, ch 2, sk ch sp, dc in dc, ch 2, sk 2 dc, dc in next dc, ch 2, sk ch sp, dc in dc; rep from * across, ending with dc in 3rd ch of ch sp at end of row, turn.

Rep Rows 2–3 to cont patt.

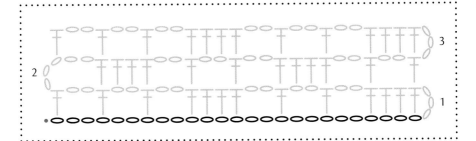

15 Eyelet Rows

Multiple of 2 stitches, plus 1

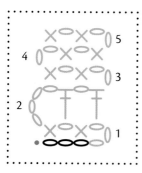

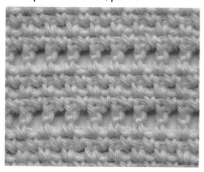

Foundation: Ch a multiple of 2 sts, plus 1, turn.

ROW 1: Ch 3, sc in 4th st from hk, *ch 1, sk 1, sc in next ch; rep from * across, turn.

ROW 2: Ch 4, dc in ch-1 sp, *ch 1, dc in next ch-1 sp; rep from * across, ending with dc in ch sp at end of row, turn.

ROW 3: Ch 2, sc in ch-1 sp, *ch 1, sc in next ch-1 sp; rep from * across, ending with sc in ch sp at end of row, turn.

ROWS 4–5: Ch 2, sc in ch-1 sp, *ch 1, sc in next ch-1 sp; rep from * across, ending with sc in ch sp at end of row, turn.

Rep Rows 2–5 to cont patt.

16 Openwork Stripes

Multiple of 2 stitches, plus 1

Foundation: Ch a multiple of 2 sts, plus 1, turn.

ROW 1: Ch 3, sc in 4th st from hk, *ch 1, sk 1, sc in next ch; rep from * across, turn.

ROW 2: Ch 4, dc in ch-1 sp, *ch 1, dc in next ch-1 sp; rep from * across, ending with dc in ch sp at end of row, turn.

ROW 3: Ch 4, dc in ch-1 sp, *ch 1, dc in next ch-1 sp; rep from * across, ending with dc in ch sp at end of row, turn.

ROW 4: Ch 2, sc in ch-1 sp, *ch 1, sc in next ch-1 sp; rep from * across, ending with sc in ch sp at end of row, turn.

ROWS 5–6: Ch 2, sc in ch-1 sp, *ch 1, sc in next ch-1 sp; rep from * across, ending with sc in ch sp at end of row, turn.

Rep Rows 2–6 to cont patt.

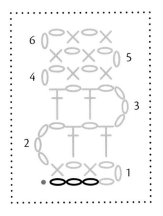

17 Mini Blocks

Reversible

Multiple of 4 stitches, plus 3

18 Vertical Stripes

Multiple of 13 stitches

Foundation: Ch a multiple of 4 sts, plus 3, turn.

ROW 1: Ch 3, sc in 6th ch from hk, sc, *ch 2, sk 2, 2 sc; rep from * to last 3 ch, ch 2, sk 2, sc, turn.

ROW 2: Ch 1, 2 sc in ch-2 sp, *ch 2, 2 sc in next ch-2 sp; rep from * across, ending with 2 sc in ch sp at end of row, turn.

ROW 3: Ch 3, 2 sc in ch-2 sp, *ch 2, 2 sc in next ch-2 sp; rep from * across, ending with ch 2, sc in ch at end of row, turn.

Rep Rows 2–3 to cont patt.

Foundation: Ch a multiple of 13 sts, turn.

ROW 1: Ch 3, dc in 4th ch from hk, 3 dc, *ch 2, sk 2, sc, ch 2, sk 2, 8 dc; rep from * across, ending with 4 dc, turn.

ROW 2: Ch 2, *4 hdc, ch 2, sk 2, tr in sc, ch 2, sk 2, 4 hdc; rep from *across, turn.

ROW 3: Ch 3, *4 dc, ch 2, sk 2, sc in tr, ch 2, sk 2, 4 dc; rep from * across, turn.

Rep Rows 2–3 to cont patt.

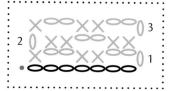

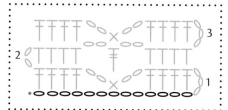

19 Windows

Multiple of 12 stitches, plus 1

Note: Rows 1 and 4 don't count the ch-3 at the beg of the row as a stitch. Rows 2 and 3 do count the first 3 ch of the ch-5 at the beg of the row as a stitch.

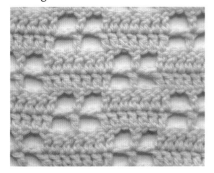

Foundation: Ch a multiple of 12 sts, plus 1, turn.

ROW 1: Ch 3, dc in 4th ch from hk, 6 dc, *ch 2, sk 2, dc, ch 2, sk 2, 7 dc; rep from * across, ending with 1 dc instead of 7 dc, turn.

ROW 2: Ch 5, sk ch sp, dc in dc, ch 2, sk ch sp, 7 dc, *ch 2, sk ch sp, dc in dc, ch 2, sk ch sp, 7 dc; rep from * across, turn.

ROW 3: Ch 5, sk 3, dc, ch 2, sk 2, 7 dc, *ch 2, sk 2, dc, ch 2, sk 2, 7 dc; rep from * across, making last 3 dc in ch at end of row, turn.

ROW 4: Ch 3, *7 dc, ch 2, sk ch sp, dc in dc, ch 2, sk ch sp; rep from * across, ending with 1 dc in 3rd ch of ch sp at end of row, turn.

ROW 5: Ch 3, *7 dc, ch 2, sk 2, dc, ch 2, sk 2; rep from * across, ending with 1 dc, turn.

Rep Rows 2–5 to cont patt.

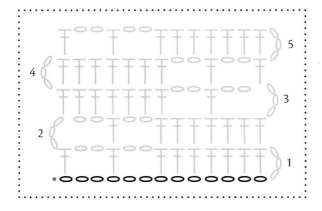

20 Diamond Lattice

Multiple of 8 stitches, plus 1

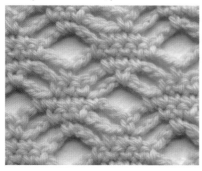

Foundation: Ch a multiple of 8 sts, plus 1, turn.

ROW 1: Ch 1, sc in 2nd ch from hk and next 2 ch, *ch 5, sk 3, 5 sc; rep from * across, ending with 3 sc instead of 5 sc, turn.

ROW 2: Ch 1, 2 sc, *ch 3, sc in ch-5 sp, ch 3, sk 1, 3 sc; rep from * across, ending with 2 sc instead of 3 sc, turn.

ROW 3: Ch 1, sc, *ch 3, sc in ch-3 sp, sc in sc, sc in ch-3 sp, ch 3, sk 1, sc in next sc; rep from * across, turn.

ROW 4: Ch 6, *sc in ch-3 sp, 3 sc, sc in ch-3 sp, ch 5; rep from * across, ending with ch 3, tr in last sc of row, instead of ch 5, turn.

ROW 5: Ch 1, sc in ch-3 sp, *ch 3, sk 1, 3 sc, ch 3, sc in ch-5 sp; rep from * across, ending with sc in ch sp at end of row instead of ch-5 sp, turn.

ROW 6: Ch 1, sc in sc, sc in ch-3 sp, *ch 3, sk 1, sc in next sc, ch 3, sc in ch-3 sp, sc in sc, sc in ch-3 sp; rep from * across, ending with ch 3, sk 1, sc in next sc, ch 3, sc in ch-3 sp, sc in last st, turn.

ROW 7: Ch 1, sc in next 2 sc, sc in ch-3 sp, *ch 5, sc in ch-3 sp, 3 sc, sc in ch-3 sp; rep from * across, ending with ch 5, sc in ch-3 sp, sc in last 2 sc, turn.

Rep Rows 2–7 to cont patt.

Shell Stitches and Shell Stitch Combinations

21 V-Stitch

Reversible
Multiple of 3 stitches, plus 1

Foundation: Ch a multiple of 3 sts, plus 1, turn.

ROW 1: Ch 2, (sc, ch 1, sc) in 3rd ch from hk, *sk 2, (sc, ch 1, sc) in next ch; rep from * across, turn.

ROW 2: Ch 2, (sc, ch 1, sc) in ea ch-1 sp across, turn.

Rep Row 2 to cont patt.

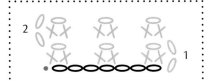

22 Open V-Stitch

Reversible
Multiple of 3 stitches, plus 1

Foundation: Ch a multiple of 3 sts, plus 1, turn.

ROW 1: Ch 3, (dc, ch 1, dc) in 4th ch from hk, *sk 2, (dc, ch 1, dc) in next ch; rep from * across, turn.

ROW 2: Ch 3, (dc, ch 1, dc) in ea ch-1 sp across, turn.

Rep Row 2 to cont patt.

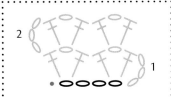

23 Open Shells

Reversible

Multiple of 4 stitches, plus 2

Foundation: Ch a multiple of 4 sts, plus 2, turn.

ROW 1: Ch 3, 2 dc in 4th ch from hk, ch 2, 2 dc in next ch, *sk 2, 2 dc in next ch, ch 2, 2 dc in next ch; rep from * across, turn.

ROW 2: Ch 3, (2 dc, ch 2, 2 dc) in ea ch-2 sp across, turn.

Rep Row 2 to cont patt.

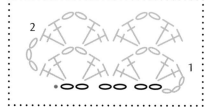

24 Stacked Shells

Reversible

Multiple of 4 stitches, plus 1

Foundation: Ch a multiple of 4 sts, plus 1, turn.

ROW 1: Ch 3, 5 dc in 4th ch from hk, *sk 3, 5 dc in next ch; rep from * across, turn.

ROW 2: Ch 3, *5 dc in 3rd dc of 5-dc shell; rep from * across, turn.

Rep Row 2 to cont patt.

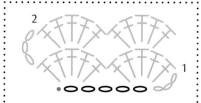

25 Open Shells

Reversible

Multiple of 6 stitches, plus 1

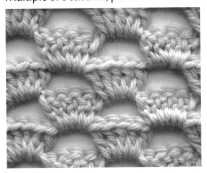

Foundation: Ch a multiple of 6 sts, plus 1, turn.

ROW 1: Ch 4, 5 dc in 5th ch from hk, *ch 2, sk 5, 5 dc in next ch; rep from * across, ending with 3 dc in last ch instead of 5 dc, turn.

ROW 2: Ch 4, *5 dc in ch-2 sp, ch 2; rep from * across, ending with 3 dc in ch sp at the end of the row, turn.

Rep Row 2 to cont patt.

26 Basic Shell Blocks

Reversible

Multiple of 4 stitches, plus 1

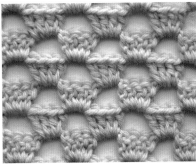

Foundation: Ch a multiple of 4 sts, plus 1, turn.

ROW 1: Ch 3, 2 dc in 4th ch from hk, 2 dc in next ch, *sk 2, ch 2, 2 dc in ea of next 2 chs; rep from * to last 3 sts, ch 2, sk 2, dc in last st, turn.

ROW 2: Ch 3, *4 dc in ch-2 sp, ch 2; rep from * across, dc in ch sp at end of row, turn.

Rep Row 2 to cont patt.

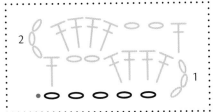

27 Clustered Shells

Reversible

Multiple of 6 stitches, plus 1

Foundation: Ch a multiple of 6 sts, plus 1, turn.

ROW 1: Ch 3, 5 dc in 4th ch from hk, *sk 2, sc, sk 2, 5 dc in next st; rep from * across, ending with 3 dc in last st instead of 5 dc, turn.

ROW 2: Ch 1, 5 dc in sc between shells, *sc in 3rd dc of 5-dc shell, 5 dc in sc between shells; rep from * across, ending with 3 dc in ch sp at the end of the row, turn.

Rep Row 2 to cont patt.

28 Shells to Clusters

Reversible

Multiple of 4 stitches, plus 1

Foundation: Ch a multiple of 4 sts, plus 1, turn.

ROW 1: Ch 3, 4 dc in 4th ch from hk, *sk 3, 4 dc in next ch; rep from * across, turn.

ROW 2: Ch 3, *make 4-dc cluster in 4-dc shell, ch 3; rep from * across, turn.

ROW 3: Ch 3, *4 dc in 4-dc cluster; rep from * across, turn.

Rep Rows 2–3 to cont patt.

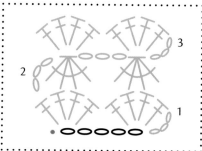

29 Open Shell Stripes

Reversible

Multiple of 5 stitches, plus 1

Foundation: Ch a multiple of 5 sts, plus 1, turn.

ROW 1: Ch 3, (2 dc, ch 2, 2 dc) in 4th ch from hk, *ch 2, sk 4, (2 dc, ch 2, 2 dc) in next ch; rep from * across, turn.

ROW 2: Ch 3, (2 dc, ch 2, 2 dc) in shell ch sp, *ch 2, (2 dc, ch 2, 2 dc) in next shell ch sp; rep from * across, turn.

Rep Row 2 to cont patt.

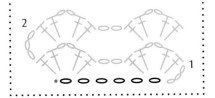

30 Divided Open Shells

Reversible

Multiple of 8 stitches, plus 1

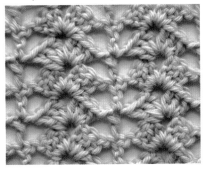

Foundation: Ch a multiple of 8 sts, plus 1, turn.

ROW 1: Ch 3, (3 dc, ch 2, 3 dc) in 4th ch from hk, *ch 1, sk 3, dc, ch 1, sk 3, (3 dc, ch 2, 3 dc) in next ch; rep from * across, turn.

ROW 2: Ch 3, (3 dc, ch 2, 3 dc) in shell ch sp, *ch 1, dc in dc, ch 1, (3 dc, ch 2, 3 dc) in shell ch sp; rep from * across, turn.

Rep Row 2 to cont patt.

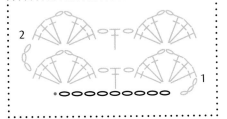

31 Scattered Shells

Multiple of 12 stitches, plus 1

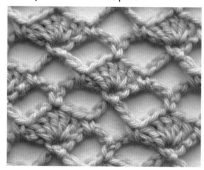

Foundation: Ch a multiple of 12 sts, plus 1, turn.

ROW 1: Ch 7, sc in 8th ch from hk, *ch 5, sk 3, sc; rep from *across, turn.

ROW 2: Ch 6, sc in ch-5 sp, 5 dc in sc, *sc in ch-5 sp, ch 5, sc in next ch-5 sp, 5 dc in sc; rep from * across, sc in 5th ch of ch sp at end of row, turn.

ROW 3: Ch 6, sc in 3rd dc of 5-dc shell, *ch 5, sc in ch-5 sp, ch 5, sc in 3rd dc of 5-dc shell; rep from * across, ch 5, sc in ch sp at end of row, turn.

ROW 4: Ch 3, 3 dc in sc, sc in ch-5 sp, ch 5, sc in ch-5 sp, *5 dc in sc, sc in ch-5 sp, ch 5, sc in ch-5 sp; rep from * across, ending with a sc in the 4th ch of ch sp at end of row, turn.

ROW 5: Ch 6, sc in ch-5 sp, *ch 5, sc in 3rd dc of 5-dc shell, ch 5, sc in ch-5 sp; rep from * ch 5, sc in ch sp at end of row, turn.

Rep Rows 2–5 to cont patt.

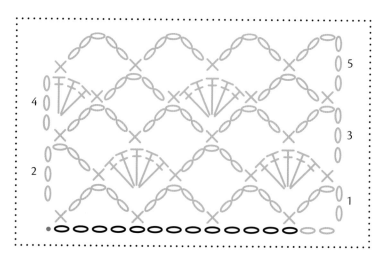

32 Diamond Shells

Multiple of 4 stitches, plus 1

Foundation: Ch a multiple of 4 sts, plus 1, turn.

ROW 1: Ch 7, sc in 8th ch from hk, *ch 5, sk 3, sc in next ch; rep from * across, turn.

ROW 2: Ch 3, 2 dc in sc, *sc in center ch of ch sp, 5 dc in sc; rep from * across, ending with a sc in the 5th ch of ch sp at end of row, turn.

ROW 3: Ch 6, sc in 3rd dc of 5-dc shell, *ch 5, sc in 3rd dc of 5-dc shell; rep from * across, ending with sc in last dc, turn.

Rep Rows 2–3 to cont patt.

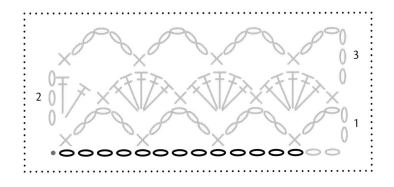

33 Offset Shells

Reversible

Multiple of 4 stitches, plus 1

Foundation: Ch a multiple of 4 sts, plus 1, turn.

ROW 1: Ch 3, (2 dc, ch 1, dc) in 4th ch from hk, *sk 3, (3 dc, ch 1, dc) in next st; rep from * across, turn.

ROW 2: Ch 3, (2 dc, ch 1, dc in ch sp, *(3 dc, ch 1, dc) in next ch sp; rep from * across, turn.

Rep Row 2 to cont patt.

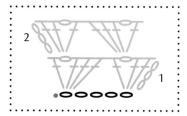

34 Mirror Offset Shells

Reversible

Multiple of 9 stitches, plus 1

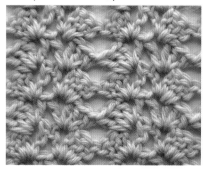

Foundation: Ch a multiple of 9 sts, plus 1, turn.

ROW 1: Ch 4, 3 dc in 5th ch from hk, *sk 5, (3 dc, ch 1, dc) in next ch, sk 2, (dc, ch 1, 3 dc) in next st; rep from * across, turn.

ROW 2: Ch 3, *(3 dc, ch 1, dc) in ch sp, (dc, ch 1, 3 dc) in next ch sp; rep from * across, (3 dc, ch 1, dc) in ch sp at end of row, turn.

ROW 3: Ch 4, 3 dc in 1st ch sp, *(3 dc, ch 1, dc) in next ch sp, (dc, ch 1, 3 dc) in next ch sp; rep from * across, turn.

Rep Rows 2–3 to cont patt.

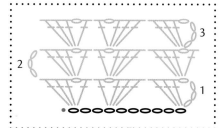

35 Lattice and Shell Rows

Multiple of 6 stitches, plus 4

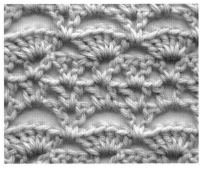

Foundation: Ch a multiple of 6 sts, plus 4, turn.

Row 1: Ch 4, dc in 5th ch from hk, *sk 2, (dc, ch 1, dc) in next ch; rep from * across, turn.

ROW 2: Ch 3, *(dc, ch 1, dc) in ch-1 sp; rep from * across, ending with last (dc, ch 1, dc) in ch sp at end of row, turn.

ROW 3: Ch 3, 6 dc in ch sp, *sk ch sp, 6 dc in next ch sp; rep from * across, turn.

ROW 4: Ch 4, dc in base of ch-4, *ch 3, sk shell, (dc, ch 1, dc) between shells; rep from * across to last shell, ch 3, sk last shell, dc in ch sp at end of row, turn.

ROW 5: Ch 3, (dc, ch 1, dc) in ch-3 sp, *(dc, ch 1, dc) in ch-1 sp, (dc, ch 1, dc) in next ch-3 sp; rep from * across to last ch-3 sp, (dc, ch 1, dc) in ch sp at end of row, turn.

ROW 6: Ch 3, *(dc, ch 1, dc) in ch-1 sp; rep from * across, turn.

Rep Rows 3–6 to cont patt.

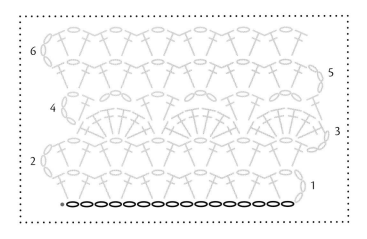

36 Latice Stripes

Multiple of 12 stitches, plus 6

Foundation: Ch a multiple of 12 sts, plus 6, turn.

ROW 1: Ch 4, dc in 6th ch from hk, *ch 1, sk 1, dc in next ch; rep from * across, turn.

ROW 2: Ch 1, sc in 1st dc, *sk ch-1 sp, 5 dc in next ch-1 sp, sk dc, sc in next dc; rep from * across, ending with a sc in 3rd ch of turning ch, turn.

ROW 3: Ch 4, sc in 3rd dc of 5-dc shell, *ch 6, sc in 3rd dc of 5-dc shell; rep from * across, ending with ch 2, dc in sc at end of row, turn.

ROW 4: Ch 1, sc in dc, *ch 6, sc in next ch-6 sp; rep from * across, ending with ch 6, sc in ch-4 at end of row, turn.

ROW 5: Ch 4, sc in ch-6 sp, *ch 6, sc in next ch-6 sp; rep from * across, ending with ch 2, dc in sc at end of row, turn.

ROW 6: Ch 1, sc in dc, 2 sc in ch-2 sp, *6 sc in ch-6 sp; rep from * across, ending with 3 sc in ch-4 sp at end of row, turn.

ROW 7: Ch 4, sk 1, dc, *ch 1, sk 1, dc; rep from * across, turn.

Rep Rows 2–7 to cont patt.

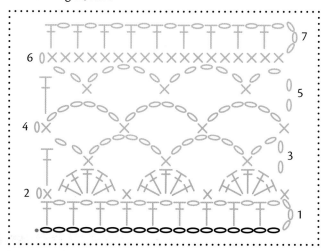

37 Trinity Shells

Multiple of 10 stitches, plus 11

Foundation: Ch a multiple of 10 sts, plus 11, turn.

ROW 1: Ch 1, sc in the 2nd ch from hk and next 2 ch, *sk 2, 7 dc in next ch, sk 2, sc in next 5 ch; rep from * across, ending with sc in last 3 ch, turn.

ROW 2: Ch 3, dc in 2nd sc, *ch 2, sc in center 3 dc of shell, ch 2, dc in center 3 dc of next 5 sc; rep from * across, ending with dc in last 2 sc of row, turn.

ROW 3: Ch 3, 3 dc in 1st dc, *sc in ch-2 sp, sc in next 3 sc, sc in next ch-2 sp, 7 dc in center dc of 3 dc; rep from * across, ending with 3 dc in ch sp at end of row, turn.

ROW 4: Ch 1, sc in 1st dc, ch 3, dc in center 3 sc of next 5 sc, *ch 2, sc in center 3 dc of next shell, ch 2, dc in center 3 sc of next 5 sc; rep from * across, ch 2, sc in last dc and 3rd ch of ch sp at end of row, turn.

ROW 5: Ch 1, sc in 1st 2 sc and in ch-2 sp, 7 dc in center dc of 3 dc, *sc in ch-2 sp, sc in next 3 sc, sc in next ch-2 sp, 7 dc in middle dc of 3 dc; rep from * across, 2 sc in last ch sp, sc in sc at end of row, turn.

Rep Rows 2–5 to cont patt.

Chevrons, Ripples and Waves

38 Classic Ripple

Reversible
Multiple of 16 stitches, plus 13

Foundation: Ch a multiple of 16 sts, plus 13, turn.

ROW 1: Ch 3, dc in the 4th ch from hk and next 4 ch, 2 dc in next ch, ch 3, sk 1, 2 dc in next ch, 5 dc, *sk 3, 5 dc, 2 dc in next ch, ch 3, sk 1, 2 dc in next ch, 5 dc; rep from * across, turn.

ROW 2: Ch 3, sk 2, 5 dc, (2 dc, ch 3, 2 dc) in ch-3 sp, 5 dc, *sk 4, 5 dc, (2 dc, ch 3, 2 dc) in ch-3 sp, 5 dc; rep from * across, dc in 3rd ch of ch sp at end of row, turn. Rep Row 2 to cont patt.

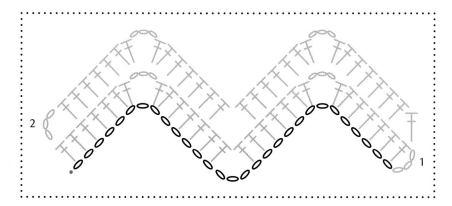

39 Mini Waves

Reversible

Multiple of 10 stitches, plus 7

Foundation: Ch a multiple of 10 sts, plus 7, turn.

ROW 1: Ch 1, sc in the 2nd ch from hk and next 2 ch, ch 3, sk 1, 3 sc, *sk 3, 3 sc, ch 3, sk 1, 3 sc; rep from * across, turn.

ROW 2: Ch 1, sk 1, 2 sc, (sc, ch 3, sc) in ch-3 sp, 2 sc, *sk 2, 2 sc, (sc, ch 3, sc) in ch-3 sp, 2 sc; rep from * across, turn.

Rep Row 2 to cont patt.

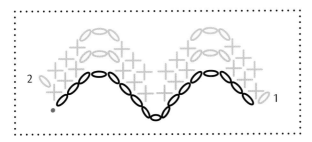

40 Eyelet Ripple

Multiple of 22 stitches, plus 19

Foundation: Ch a multiple of 22 sts, plus 19, turn.

ROW 1: Ch 3, dc in the 4th ch from hk and next ch, ch 2, sk 2, 2 dc, ch 2, sk 2, 2 dc in next ch, ch 3, sk 1, 2 dc in next ch, (ch 2, sk 2, 2 dc) twice, *sk 3, (2 dc, ch 2, sk 2) twice, 2 dc in next ch, ch 3, sk 1, 2 dc in next ch, (ch 2, sk 2, 2 dc) twice; rep from * across, turn.

ROW 2: Ch 3, 2 dc in ch-2 sp, ch 2, 2 dc in next ch-2 sp, ch 2, (2 dc, ch 3, 2 dc) in ch-3 sp, (ch 2, 2dc in ch-2 sp) twice, *2 dc in next ch-2 sp, ch 2, 2 dc in next ch-2 sp, ch 2, (2 dc, ch 3, 2 dc) in ch-3 sp, (ch 2, 2 dc in ch-2 sp) twice; rep from * across, turn.

ROW 3: Ch 3, sk 2, dc in next 8 sts and chs, 7 dc in ch-3 sp, dc in next 8 sts and chs, *4-dc cluster in next 4 sts, dc in next 8 sts and chs, 7 dc in ch-3 sp, dc in next 8 sts and chs; rep from * across, turn.

ROW 4: Ch 3, sk 2, (2 dc, ch 2, sk 2) twice, 2 dc in next st, ch 3, sk 1, 2 dc in next st, (ch 2, sk 2, 2 dc) twice, *sk 4, (2 dc, ch 2, sk 2) twice, 2 dc in next st, ch 3, sk 1, 2 dc in next st, (ch 2, sk 2, 2 dc) twice; rep from * across, turn.

Rep Rows 2–4 to cont patt.

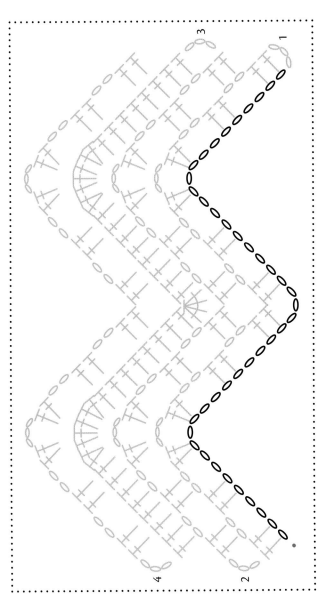

41 Solid Ripple

Reversible

Multiple of 22 stitches, plus 17

Foundation: Ch a multiple of 22 sts, plus 17, turn.

ROW 1: Ch 3, dc in 4th ch from hk and next 6 ch, 2 dc in next ch, 3 dc in next ch, 2 dc in next ch, 7 dc, *5-dc cluster in next 5 ch, 7 dc, 2 dc in next ch, 3 dc in next ch, 2 dc in next ch, 7 dc; rep from * across, turn.

ROW 2: Ch 1, sc in ea st across, turn.

ROW 3: Ch 3, sk 2, 7 dc, 2 dc in next st, 3 dc in next st, 2 dc in next st, 7 dc, *5-dc cluster in next 5 sts, 7 dc, 2 dc in next sc, 3 dc in next sc, 2 dc in next sc, 7 dc; rep from * across, turn.

Rep Rows 2-3 to cont patt.

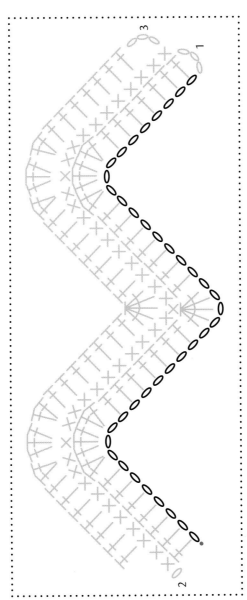

42 Ocean Swells

Multiple of 28 stitches, plus 1

Foundation: Ch a multiple of 28 sts, plus 1, turn.

ROW 1: Ch 1, sc in the 2nd ch from hk and the next 4 ch, hdc, dc, tr, dc, hdc, *9 sc, hdc, dc, tr, dc, hdc; rep from * across, ending with 5 sc, turn.

ROW 2: Ch 1, 3 sc, *ch 1, sk 2, dc, (ch 1, dc) 4 times, ch 1, sk 2, 5 sc; rep from * across, ending with 3 sc instead of 5 sc, turn.

ROWS 3 AND 11: *(2 dc in next ch sp) twice, 3 dc in next ch sp, dc in dc, 3 dc in next ch sp, (2 dc in next ch sp) twice, sk 2 sc, sc in next sc, sk 2 sc; rep from * across, sc in last st in row, turn.

ROW 4: Ch 1, sc in ea st across, turn.

ROW 5: Ch 4, dc in 1st st, hdc in next st, sk 1, sc in next 9 sts, *sk 1, hdc, dc, tr, dc, hdc, sk 1, sc in next 9 sc; rep from * across, sk 1, hdc, dc, tr, turn.

ROW 6: Ch 4, dc in dc, ch 1, dc in hdc, *ch 1, sk 2, sc in next 5 sc, ch 1, sk 2, (dc, ch 1) 5 times, sk 2, sc in next 5 sc; rep from * across, sk 2, ch 1, dc in hdc, ch 1, dc in dc, ch 1, dc in 4th ch of ch sp at end of row, turn.

ROW 7: Ch 3, (2 dc in next ch sp) 3 times, sk 2, sc, *sk 2, (2 dc in next ch sp) twice, 3 dc in next ch sp, dc in next dc, 3 dc in next ch sp, (2 dc in next ch sp) twice, sk 2, sc; rep from * across, sk 2, (2 dc in next ch sp) twice, 3 dc in ch sp at end of row, dc in 3rd ch of ch sp at end of row, turn.

ROW 8: Ch 1, sk 1, sc in ea st across, ending with sc in ch sp at end of row, turn.

ROW 9: Ch 1, sc in next 4 sc, *sk 1, hdc, dc, tr, dc, hdc, sk 1, sc in next 9 sc; rep from * across, ending with 4 sc instead of 9 sc, turn.

ROW 10: Ch 1, sc in next 2 sc, *ch 1, sk 2, (dc, ch 1) 5 times, sk 2, sc in next 5 sc; rep from * across, ending with 2 sc instead of next 5 sc, turn.

Rep Rows 4–11 to cont patt.

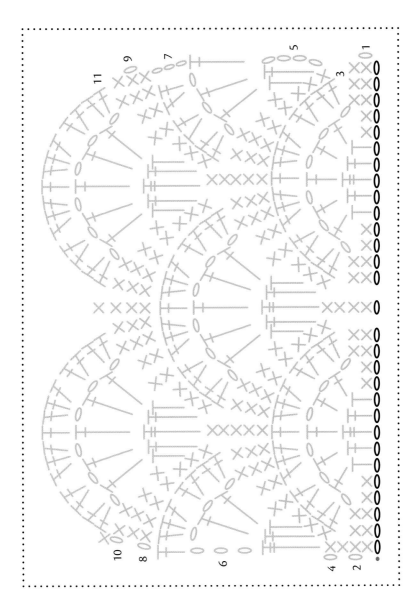

43 Shamrock Ripple

Multiple of 16 stitches, plus 13

Foundation: Ch a multiple of 16 sts, plus 13, turn.

ROW 1: Ch 3, dc in the 4th ch from hk and next 4 ch, ch 3, sk 1, sc, ch 3, sk 1, 5 dc, *sk 3, 5 dc, ch 3, sk 1, sc, ch 3, sk 1, 5 dc; rep from * across, turn.

ROW 2: Ch 3, sk 2, 3 dc, 4 dc in ch-3 sp, ch 3, 4 dc in next ch-3 sp, 3 dc, *sk 4, 3 dc, 4 dc in ch-3 sp, ch 3, 4 dc in next ch-3 sp, 3 dc; rep from * across, turn.

ROW 3: Ch 3, sk2, 5 dc, 7 dc in ch-3 sp, 5 dc, *sk 4, 5 dc, 7 dc in ch-3 sp, 5 dc; rep from * across, turn.

ROW 4: Ch 3, sk 2, 6 dc, 5 dc in next dc, 6 dc, *sk 4, 6 dc, 5 dc in next dc, 6 dc; rep from * across, turn.

ROW 5: Ch 3, sk 2, 5 dc, ch 3, sk 1, sc, ch 3, sk 1, 5 dc, *sk 4, 5 dc, ch 3, sk 1, sc, ch 3, sk 1, 5 dc; rep from * across, turn.

Rep Rows 2-5 to cont patt.

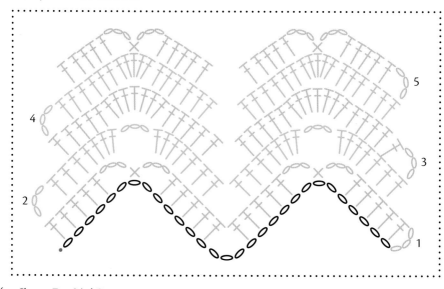

Stretched Stitches

44 Stretched Single Crochet

Multiple of 2 stitches, plus 3

Foundation: Ch a multiple of 2 sts, plus 3, turn.

ROW 1: Ch 1, sc in the 2nd ch from hk and ea ch across, turn.

ROW 2: Ch 1, sc in ea st across, turn.

ROW 3: Ch 1, *sc, sc in row below; rep from * across sc, turn.

Rep Rows 2–3 to cont patt.

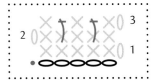

45 Slant

Multiple of 4 stitches, plus 1

Foundation: Ch a multiple of 4 sts, plus 1, turn.

ROW 1: Ch 1, sc in the 2nd ch from hk and ea ch across, turn.

ROWS 2, 4 AND 5: Ch 1, sc in ea st across, turn.

ROW 3: Ch 1, *3 sc, sc in row below and 3 sts to the right; rep from * to last st, sc, turn.

Rep Rows 2–5 to cont patt.

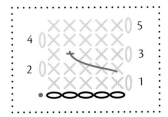

46 Stretched ZigZag

Multiple of 4 stitches, plus 3

Foundation: Ch a multiple of 4 sts, plus 3, turn.

ROW 1: Ch 2, hdc in the 3rd ch from hk and ea ch across, turn.

ROWS 2, 4 AND 6: Ch 2, hdc in ea st across, turn.

ROW 3: Ch 1, 2 sc, sc in row below, *3 sc, sc in row below; rep from * across, turn.

ROW 5: Ch 1, *sc, sc in row below; rep from * to last st, sc, turn.

ROW 7: Ch 1, sc in row below, *3 sc, sc in row below; rep from * to last 2 sts, 2 sc, turn.

Use as a border, or rep Rows 2–7 to cont patt.

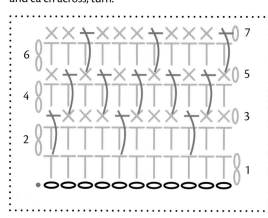

47 Grouped Threes

Multiple of 6 stitches, plus 3

Foundation: Ch a multiple of 6 sts, plus 3, turn.

ROW 1: Ch 1, sc in the 2nd ch from hk and ea ch across, turn.

ROWS 2 AND 4: Ch 2, hdc in ea st across, turn.

ROW 3: Ch 1, *3 sc, sc in row below, sc 2 rows below, sc in row below; rep from * to last 3 sts, 3 sc, turn.

ROW 5: Ch 1, sc in ea st across, turn.

Rep Rows 2–5 to cont patt.

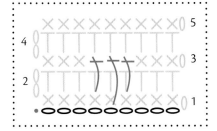

48 Three Double Crochet Wrap

Multiple of 4 stitches, plus 1

Foundation: Ch a multiple of 4 sts, plus 1, turn.

ROW 1: Ch 1, sc in the 2nd ch from hk and ea ch across, turn.

ROW 2: Ch 3, *sk 1, 3 dc, dc in skipped st; rep from * across, turn.

ROW 3: Ch 1, sc in ea st across and in ch sp at end of row, turn.

Rep Rows 2–3 to cont patt.

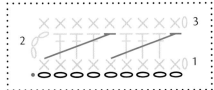

49 Back and Forth

Multiple of 5 stitches

Foundation: Ch a multiple of 5 sts, turn.

ROW 1: Ch 1, sc in the 2nd ch from hk and ea ch across, turn.

ROWS 2, 3, 5 AND 6: Ch 1, sc in ea st across, turn.

ROW 4: Ch 1, *3 sc, sc in row below and 3 sts to the left; rep from * to last st, sc, turn.

ROW 7: Ch 1, *3 sc, sc in row below and 3 sts to the right; rep from * to last st, sc, turn.

Rep Rows 2–7 to cont patt.

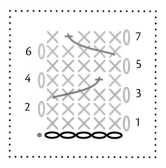

Post Stitches

50 Single Crochet Post Weave

Reversible

Multiple of 2 stitches

Foundation: Ch a multiple of 2 sts, turn.

ROW 1: Ch 1, sc in 2nd ch from hk and ea ch across, turn.

ROW 2: Ch 1, *FPsc, BPsc; rep from * across, turn.

ROW 3: Ch 1, *BPsc, FPsc; rep from * across, turn.

Rep Rows 2–3 to cont patt.

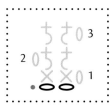

51 Single Crochet Post Rows

Multiple of 2 stitches

Foundation: Ch a multiple of 2 sts, turn.

ROW 1: Ch 1, sc in the 2nd ch from hk and ea ch across, turn.

ROW 2: Ch 1, *FPsc, BPsc; rep from * across, turn.

Rep Row 2 to cont patt.

52 Double Crochet Post Rows

Reversible

Any number of stitches

Foundation: Ch any number of sts, turn.

ROW 1: Ch 3, dc in 4th ch from hk and ea ch across, turn.

ROW 2: Ch 3, FPdc in ea st across, turn.

Rep Row 2 to cont patt.

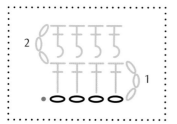

53 Post Ribbing

Reversible

Multiple of 2 stitches

Foundation: Ch a multiple of 2 sts, turn.

ROW 1: Ch 3, dc in 4th ch from hk and ea ch across, turn.

ROW 2: Ch 3, (FPdc, BPdc) rep across, turn.

Rep Row 2 to cont patt.

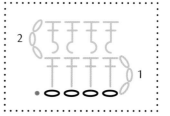

54 Post Stripes

Multiple of 4 stitches, plus 3

Foundation: Ch a multiple of 4 sts, plus 3, turn.

ROW 1: Ch 3, dc in 4th ch from hk and ea ch across, turn.

ROW 2: Ch 3, *3 dc, BPdc; rep from * to last 3 sts, 3 dc, turn.

ROW 3: Ch 3, *3 dc, FPdc; rep from * to last 3 sts, 3 dc, turn.

Rep Rows 2–3 to cont patt.

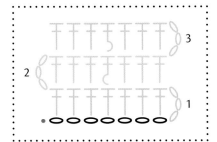

55 Post Leaning Stripe

Multiple of 4 stitches, plus 1

Foundation: Ch a multiple of 4 sts, plus 1, turn.

ROW 1: Ch 3, dc in 4th ch from hk and ea ch across, turn.

ROW 2: Ch 3, dc, *BPdc, 3 dc; rep from * across, turn.

ROW 3: Ch 3, 2 dc, *FPdc, 3 dc; rep from * across, ending with 2 dc instead of 3 dc, turn.

ROW 4: Ch 3, *3 dc, BPdc; rep from * to last st, dc, turn.

Rep Rows 2–4 to cont patt.

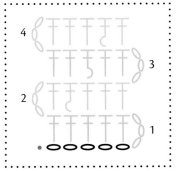

56 Post Basket Weave

Reversible

Multiple of 4 stitches, plus 2

Foundation: Ch a multiple of 4 sts, plus 2, turn.

ROW 1: Ch 2, hdc in 3rd ch from hk and ea ch across, turn.

ROWS 2 AND 3: Ch 3, dc, *2 BPdc, 2 FPdc; rep from * to last st, dc, turn.

ROWS 4 AND 5: Ch 3, dc, *2 FPdc, 2 BPdc; rep from * to last st, dc, turn.

Rep Rows 2–5 to cont patt.

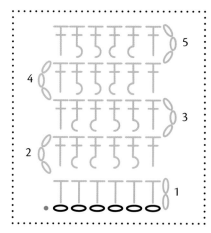

57 Posts and Vs

Multiple of 4 stitches, plus 3

Foundation: Ch a multiple of 4 sts, plus 3, turn.

ROW 1: Ch 3, dc in 4th ch from hk, dc, *sk 1, (dc, ch 1, dc) in next ch, sk 1, dc; rep from * to last ch, dc, turn.

ROW 2: Ch 3, dc, BPdc, *(dc, ch 1, dc) in ch-1 sp, BPdc; rep from * to last st, dc, turn.

ROW 3: Ch 3, dc, FPdc, *(dc, ch 1, dc) in ch-1 sp, FPdc; rep from * to last st, dc, turn.

Rep Rows 2–3 to cont patt.

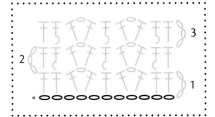

58 Small Cable Post

Multiple of 5 stitches, plus 3

Foundation: Ch a multiple of 5 sts, plus 3, turn.

ROW 1: Ch 3, dc in 4th ch from hk and ea ch across, turn.

ROW 2: Ch 3, *3 dc, 2 BPdc; rep from * to last 3 sts, 3 dc, turn.

ROW 3: Ch 3, *3 dc, sk 1, FPdc, FPdc in skipped st; rep from * to last 3 sts, 3 dc, turn.

Rep Rows 2–3 to cont patt.

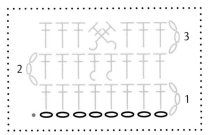

Clusters, Bobbles and Popcorns

59 Clusters

Reversible

Multiple of 2 stitches, plus 1

Foundation: Ch a multiple of 2 sts, plus 1, turn.

ROW 1: Ch 4, 3-dc cluster in 5th ch from hk, *ch 1, sk 1, 3-dc cluster in next ch; rep from * across, turn.

ROW 2: Ch 4, 3-dc cluster in next ch-1 sp, *ch 1, 3-dc cluster in next ch-1 sp; rep from * across, ch 1, 3-dc cluster in ch sp at end of row, turn.

Rep Row 2 to cont patt.

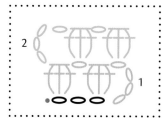

60 Cluster Stripes

Multiple of 7 stitches

Foundation: Ch a multiple of 7 sts, turn.

ROW 1: Ch 4, 3-dc cluster in 6th ch from hk, ch 1, sk 1, 4 dc, *ch 1, sk 1, 3-dc cluster in next ch, ch 1, sk 1, 4 dc; rep from * across, turn.

ROW 2: Ch 3, *3 dc, ch 1, 3-dc cluster in ch-1 sp, ch 1, dc in next ch-1 sp; rep from * across, ending with dc in ch sp at end of row, turn.

ROW 3: Ch 4, 3-dc cluster in ch-1 sp, ch 1, dc in next ch-1 sp, 3 dc, *ch 1, 3-dc cluster in ch-1 sp, ch 1, dc in next ch-1 sp, 3 dc; rep from * across, turn.

Rep Rows 2–3 to cont patt.

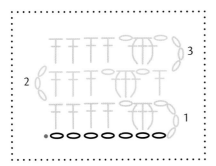

61 Cluster Lattice

Multiple of 7 stitches

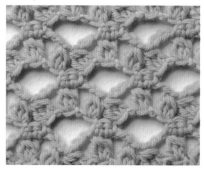

Foundation: Ch a multiple of 7 sts, turn.

ROW 1: Ch 3, dc in 4th ch from hk and ea ch across, turn.

ROW 2: Ch 1, 2 sc, *ch 5, sk 3, 4 sc; rep from * across, ending with 2 sc instead of 4 sc, turn.

ROW 3: Ch 2, (3-dc cluster, ch 3, 3-dc cluster, ch 3, 3-dc cluster) in each ch-5 sp across, dc in ch sp at end of row, turn.

ROW 4: Ch 7, sc in first ch-3 sp, sc in next cluster, sc in next ch-3 sp, *ch 5, sc in next ch-3 sp, sc in next cluster, sc in ch-3 sp; rep from * across, ch 2, tr in ch sp at end of row, turn.

ROW 5: Ch 3, dc in tr, ch 3, 3-dc cluster in ch-2 sp, *(3-dc cluster, ch 3, 3-dc cluster, ch 3, 3-dc cluster) in ch-5 sp; rep from * across, ending with (3-dc cluster, ch 3, 3 dc cluster) in ch sp at end of row, turn.

ROW 6: Ch 1, sc in first cluster, sc in next ch-3 sp, ch 5, *sc in next ch-3 sp, sc in next cluster, sc in ch-3 sp, ch 5; rep from * across, sc in last ch-3 sp, sc in dc, turn.

Rep Rows 3–6 to cont patt.

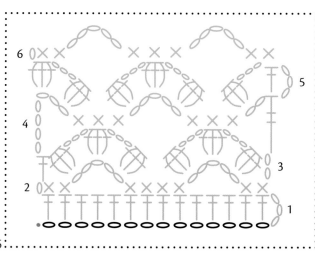

62 Popcorn Grid

Multiple of 3 stitches, plus 2

Foundation: Ch a multiple of 3 sts, plus 2, turn.

ROW 1: Ch 2, dc in 3rd ch from hk and ea ch across, turn.

ROW 2: Ch 2, 2 dc, *make a 5-dc popcorn, 2 dc; rep from * across, turn.

ROW 3: Ch 2, dc in ea st across, turn.

Rep Rows 2–3 to cont patt.

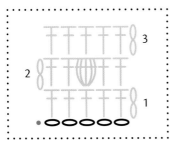

63 Popcorn Stripes

Multiple of 6 stitches, plus 5

Foundation: Ch a multiple of 6 sts, plus 5, turn.

ROW 1: Ch 2, dc in 3rd ch from hk and next 4 ch, *make a 5-dc popcorn, 5 dc; rep from * across, turn.

ROW 2: Ch 1, sc in ea st across, turn.

ROW 3: Ch 2, 5 dc, *make a 5-dc popcorn, 5 dc; rep from * across, turn.

Rep Rows 2–3 to cont patt.

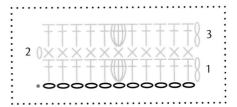

64 Allover Popcorns

Multiple of 4 stitches, plus 2

Foundation: Ch a multiple of 4 sts, plus 2, turn.

ROW 1: Ch 3, dc in 4th ch from hk and next ch, *make a 5-dc popcorn, 5 dc; rep from * across, ending with 3 dc instead of 5 dc, turn.

ROWS 2 AND 4: Ch 3, dc in ea st across, turn.

ROW 3: Ch 3, 5 dc, *make a 5-dc popcorn, 5 dc; rep from * across, ending with a 5-dc popcorn, turn.

ROW 5: Ch 3, 2 dc *make a 5-dc popcorn, 5 dc; rep from * across, ending with 3 dc instead of 5 dc, turn.

Rep Rows 2–5 to cont patt.

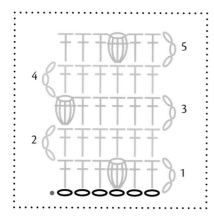

65 Popcorn Diamonds

Multiple of 11 stitches

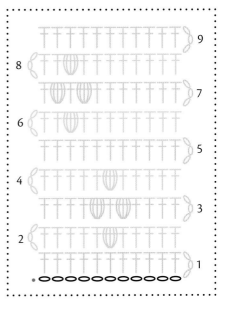

Foundation: Ch a multiple of 11 sts, turn.

ROW 1: Ch 3, dc in 4th ch from hk and ea ch across, turn.

ROWS 2 AND 4: Ch 3, 5 dc, *make a 5-dc popcorn, 10 dc; rep from * across, ending with 5 dc instead of 10 dc, turn.

ROW 3: Ch 3, 4 dc, make a 5-dc popcorn, dc in popcorn from previous row, make a 5-dc popcorn, 8 dc; rep from * across, ending with 4 dc instead of 8 dc, turn.

ROWS 5 AND 9: Ch 3, dc in ea st across, turn.

ROWS 6 AND 8: Ch 3, 2 dc, *make a 5-dc popcorn, 10 dc; rep from * across, ending with 8 dc instead of 10 dc, turn.

ROW 7: Ch 3, 7 dc, *make a 5-dc popcorn, dc in popcorn from previous row, make a 5-dc popcorn, 8 dc; rep from * across, ending with 1 dc instead of 8 dc, turn.

Rep Rows 2–9 to cont patt.

66 Popcorns and Shells

Multiple of 6 stitches, plus 4

Foundation: Ch a multiple of 6 sts, plus 4, turn.

ROW 1: Ch 4, make a 5 dc popcorn in 6th ch from hk, *ch 1, sk 2, 3 dc in next ch, ch 1, sk 2, make a 5 dc popcorn; rep from * to last 2 chs, ch 1, sk 1, dc in last ch, turn.

ROWS 2 AND 4: Ch 1, sc in ea dc, ch sp and popcorn across, sc in ch sp at end of row, turn.

ROW 3: Ch 4, sk 1, make a 5 dc popcorn, *ch 1, sk 2, 3 dc in next sc, ch 1, sk 2, make a 5 dc popcorn; rep from * to last 2 sts, ch 1, sk 1, dc in last st, turn.

Rep Rows 3–4 to cont patt.

Ruffles and Cords

67 Single Crochet Tape

Any number of stitches. The number of stitches determines the length of the cord.

Foundation: Ch any number of sts, turn.
ROW 1: Ch 1, sc in 2nd ch from hk and ea ch across.

68 Slip Stitch Cord

Any number of stitches. The number of stitches determines the diameter of the cord.

Foundation: Ch any number of sts, do not turn.
RND 1: Sl st in the last ch (next to the slip knot) to from a circle, sl st in the next 2 chs, work in the direction shown in the illustration.
Continue working a sl st in each stitch until the cord is the length intended.

69 Single Crochet Tube

Any number of stitches. The number of stitches determines the diameter of the cord.

Foundation: Ch any number of sts, do not turn.

RND 1: Join foundation into a circle with a sc in the first ch. Sc in ea st until the tube is as long as intended.

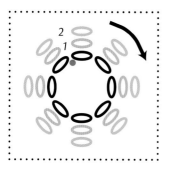

70 Single Crochet Corkscrew

Any number of stitches. The number of stitches determines the length of the cord.

Foundation: Ch any number of sts, turn.

ROW 1: Ch 1, 2 sc in 2nd ch from hk and ea ch across.

71 Reverse Single Crochet Edging

Any number of stitches. The number of stitches determines the length of the edging.

Foundation: Ch any number of sts, turn.
ROW 1: Ch 3, dc in 4th ch from hk and ea ch across, do not turn.
ROW 2: Ch 1, sc in ea st from left to right.

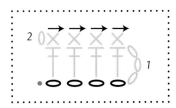

72 Ruffled Spiral

Any number of stitches. The number of stitches determines the length of the cord.

Foundation: Ch any number of sts, turn.
ROW 1: Ch 3, 4 dc in 4th ch from hk and ea ch across.

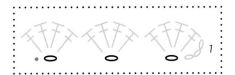

73 Loop Texture

Note: This edging is attached to fabric made up from at least one row of double crochet. The chart below shows the edging attached to four rows of double crochet.

Attach the yarn to the right corner stitch of the last row of the crocheted fabric.

ROW 1: Ch 6, sc around the post of the next st, *ch 5, sc around the post of the next st; rep from * across, turn.

ROW 2: Ch 5, sc around the post of the st at the beg of the row, *ch 5, sc around the post of the next st in the row; rep from * across, turn.

Rep Row 2 to cont patt.

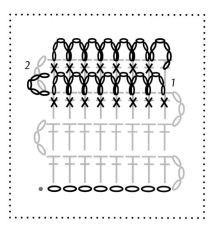

74 Wavy Ruffle Surface

Note: This edging is attached to fabric made up from at least three rows of double crochet. The chart below shows the edging attached to four rows of double crochet. In the instructions below, the last row of the fabric is referred to as Row 4, the second-to-last row is referred to as Row 3 and the third-to-last row is referred to as Row 2.

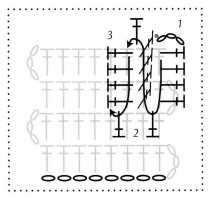

Attach the yarn to the right corner stitch of the last row of the crocheted fabric.

ROW 1: Ch 3, 2 dc around the post of the rightmost st in row 4, 2 dc around the post of the rightmost st in row 3, rotate the fabric 90 degrees, dc between the rightmost st in Row 2 and the st next to it.

ROW 2: Rotate the fabric 90 degrees so you are working in the next st from the opposite direction from the previous row of sts. 2 dc in the next st in Row 3, 2 dc in the next st in Row 4. Rotate the work 90 degrees, dc in the edge of the piece.

ROW 3: Rotate the work 90 degrees so you are working in the next row of sts in the opposite direction from the previous row. 2 dc in the next st in Row 4, 2 dc in the next st in Row 3, rotate the work 90 degrees, dc between the sts of Row 2.

Rep Rows 2–3 to cont patt.

75 Basic Ruffle

Any number of stitches. The number of stitches determines the length of the edging.

Foundation: Ch any number of sts, turn.

ROW 1: Ch 3, dc in 4th ch from hk and ea ch across, turn.

ROW 2: Ch 3, 2 dc in ea st across, turn.

ROW 3: Ch 3, dc in ea st across.

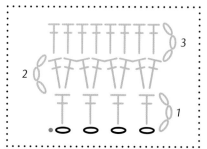

76 Looped Ruffle

Any number of stitches. The number of stitches determines the length of the edging.

Foundation: Ch any number of sts, turn.

ROW 1: Ch 3, dc in 4th ch from hk and ea ch across, turn.

ROW 2: Ch 3, 2 dc in ea st across, turn.

ROW 3: Ch 3, *dc, ch 3, dc; rep from * across.

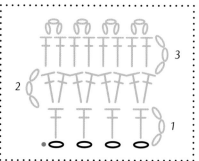

77 Picot Fan Ruffle

Multiple of 6 stitches, plus 1

Foundation: Ch a multiple of 6 sts, plus 1, turn.

ROW 1: Ch 3, dc in 4th ch from hk and ea ch across, turn.

ROW 2: Ch 1, 2 sc, *sk 1, 6 dc in next st, sk 1, 3 sc; rep from * across, ending with 2 sc instead of 3 sc, turn.

ROW 3: Ch 1, sc, *sk 1, (dc, ch 3, sl st in 3rd ch from hk, dc) in ea st of shell, sk 1, sc; rep from * across.

Leaves and Flowers

78 Violet Leaf

Foundation: Ch 1, turn.

ROW 1: Ch 4, (dc, tr, dtr, ch 3, sl st in 3rd ch from hk, dtr, tr, dc) in 4th ch from hk, ch 3, sl st in base of leaf.

79 Eucalyptus Leaf

Foundation: Ch 10, turn.

ROW 1: Ch 1, working in back loop of ea ch, sl st in 2nd and 3rd ch from hook, sc in next 2 ch, hdc in next 2 ch, dc in next 3 ch, 10 tr in last ch, rotate work and dc in front loop of next 3 ch, hdc in next 2 ch, sc in next ch, sl st in next ch.

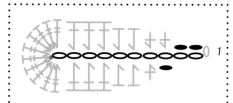

80 Ivy Leaf

Foundation: Ch 1, do not turn.

ROW 1: Ch 3, 6 dc in 4th ch from hk, turn.

ROW 2: Ch 3, 3 dc, 2 dc in next st, 2 dc, 2 dc in ch sp at end of row, turn.

ROW 3: Ch 3, 4 dc, 3 dc in next st, 4 dc, 2 dc in ch sp at end of row, turn.

ROW 4: Ch 3, 6 dc, (2 dc in next st) twice, 5 dc, dc in ch sp at end of row, turn.

ROW 5: Ch 3, 7 dc, (2 dc in next st) twice, 7 dc, dc in ch sp at end of row, turn.

ROW 6: Ch 1, sk 1, 5 sl st, ch 3, 9 dc, turn.

ROW 7: Ch 3, sk 1, 2-dc cluster, 4 dc, 2-dc cluster, turn.

ROW 8: Ch 3, sk 1, 2-dc cluster, dc, 2-dc cluster, turn.

ROW 9: Ch 3, 3-dc cluster.

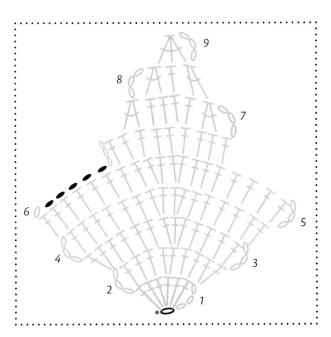

81 Grape Leaf

Foundation: Ch 14, turn.

ROW 1: Ch1, sc in back loop of second ch from hk and next 12 ch, 5 sc in last ch, sc in front loop of next 10 ch, turn.

ROW 2: Ch 1, sk 1, 10 sc, (2 sc in next st) 3 times, 10 sc, turn.

ROW 3: Ch 1, sk 1, 11 sc, (2 sc in next st) 3 times, 9 sc, turn.

ROW 4: Ch 1, sk 1, 10 sc, (2 sc in next st) 3 times, 10 sc, turn.

ROW 5: Ch 3, 12 dc, ch 1, sc in side of last dc, 2 sc, ch 3, 12dc, dc in ch sp at end of row, turn.

ROW 6: Ch 1, sk 1, 4 sl st, ch 4, tr in same st as sl st, 2 tr, 6 dc, ch 1, 3 sc along side of dc and ch-3 of previous row, 4 sc, ch 3, 5 dc, 4 tr.

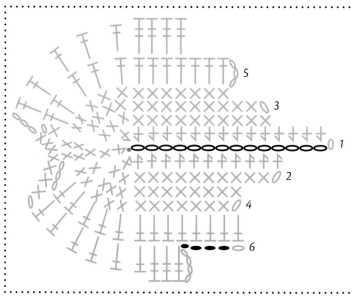

82 Oak Leaf

Foundation: Ch 1, do not turn.

ROW 1: Ch 3, dc in 4th ch from hk, turn.

ROW 2: Ch 3, dc in dc, turn.

ROW 3: Ch 3, dc in dc, dc in ch sp at end of row, turn.

ROW 4: Ch 6, dc in 3rd ch from hk and next 3 ch, dc in next 2 sts, dc in ch sp at end of row, turn.

ROWS 5–9: Ch 6, dc in 3rd ch from hk and next 3 ch, dc in next 4 sts, turn.

ROW 10: Ch 3, 3 dc, turn.

ROW 11: Ch 3, sk 1, 3-dc cluster.

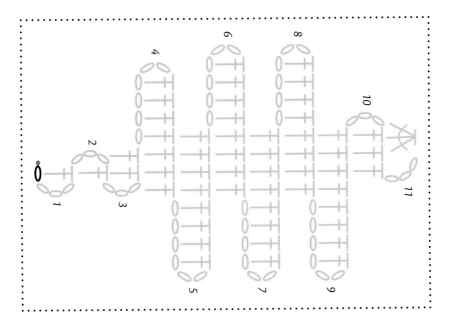

83 Ruffle Flower

Foundation: Ch 15, turn.

ROW 1: Ch 5, sc in 6th ch from hk, *ch 5, sc in next ch; rep from * 5 times. Ch5, sc in ch with first 5-ch loop to group the loops together, sc in middle of looped ch to make a ball.

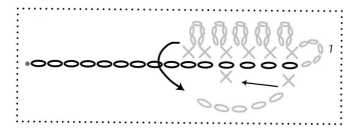

84 Spider Mum

Foundation: Ch 1, do not turn.

ROW 1: Ch 3 (counts as dc), 11 dc in 4th ch from hk, sl st in ch sp at end of row, do not turn.

ROW 2: *Ch 11, turn, sc in 2nd ch from hk and next 9 ch, sc in next st on row 1; rep from * in ea dc in Row 1 and in the ch sp at end of row.

ROW 3: Ch 6, sc in nearest post of Row 1, *ch 5, sc in next post in Row 1; rep from * in ea st in Row 1, working around twice.

123

85 Basic Flower

Made using yarn in 2 colors, Yarn A and Yarn B.

Center (Yarn A)

Ch 4, 11 dc in 4th ch from hk, sl st in the top of ch-4.

Make 2 and stitch together along the edges, stuffing the middle with the tails of yarn so the center puffs out slightly. Weave in ends.

Petals (Yarn B)

Attach Yarn B to a stitch along the edge of the Center.

ROW 1: (Ch 3, sk 1, sc) 6 times, do not turn.

ROW 2: *Ch 3, (dc, tr, dtr, ch 3, sl st in 3rd ch from hk, dtr, tr, dc) in ch-3 sp, ch 3, sl st in same ch-3 sp; rep from * in ea ch-3 sp from Row 1.

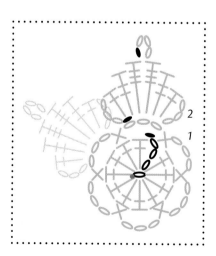

Blocks

86 Small Five-Sided Block

Foundation: Ch 5, do not turn.

RND 1: 14 tr in 5th ch from hk, sl st in top of ch-5 sp, do not turn.

RND 2: Ch 2, hdc, 2 hdc in next 2 sts, *ch 2, 2 hdc in next 3 sts; rep from * around, ch 2, sl st in top of ch-2.

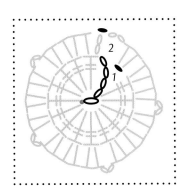

87 Small Square

Foundation: Ch 20 sts, turn.

ROW 1: Ch 3, dc in 4th ch from hk and next 7 ch, sk 3, dc in rem 9 ch, turn.

ROW 2: Ch 3, sk 1, 6 dc, sk 4, 6 dc, dc in top of ch sp at end of row, turn.

ROW 3: Ch 3, sk 1, 4 dc, sk 4, 4 dc, dc in top of ch sp at end of row, turn.

ROW 4: Ch 3, sk 1, 2 dc, sk 4, 2 dc, dc in top of ch sp at end of row, turn.

ROW 5: Ch 3, dc in ch-3 at end of row.

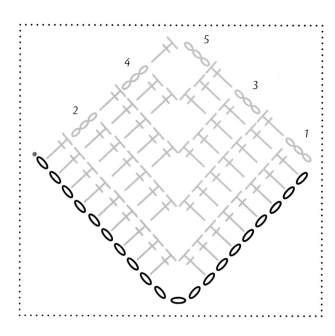

88 Classic Block

Foundation: Ch 1, do not turn.

RND 1: Ch 3, then work foll sts in the 4th ch from the hk; 3 dc, ch 2, 4 dc, ch 2, 4 dc, ch 2, 4 dc, ch 2, sl st in the top of ch-3, do not turn.

RND 2: Ch 3, *ch 2, (4 dc, ch 2, 4 dc) in next ch sp; rep from * 3 times, ch 2, (4 dc, ch 2, 3 dc) in next ch sp, sl st in top of ch-3, do not turn.

RND 3: Ch 3, 3 dc in ch-2 sp, ch 2, (4 dc, ch 2, 4 dc) in next ch-2 sp, *ch 2, 4 dc in next ch-2 sp, ch 2, (4 dc, ch 2, 4 dc) in corner ch-2 sp); rep from * 3 times, ch 2, sl st in top of ch-3 sp.

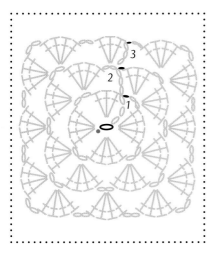

89 Triangle Block

Foundation: Ch 1, do not turn.

RND 1: Ch 3, then work foll sts in the 4th ch from the hk; 3 dc, ch 2, 4 dc, ch 2, 4 dc, ch 2, sl st in the top of ch-3, do not turn.

RND 2: Ch 3, *ch 2, (4 dc, ch 2, 4 dc) in next ch sp; rep from * twice, ch 2, (4 dc, ch 2, 3 dc) in next ch sp, sl st in top of ch-3, do not turn.

RND 3: Ch 3, 3 dc in ch-2 sp, ch 2, (4 dc, ch 2, 4 dc) in next ch-2 sp, *ch 2, 4 dc in next ch-2 sp, ch 2, (4 dc, ch 2, 4 dc) in next ch-2 sp; rep from * twice, ch 2, sl st in top of ch-3 sp.

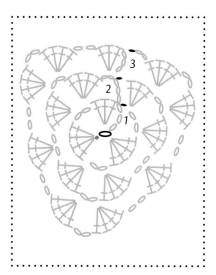

90 Five Sided Block

Foundation: Ch 1, do not turn.

RND 1: Ch 3, then work foll sts in the 4th ch from the hk; 2 dc, (ch 2, 3 dc) 4 times, ch 2, sl st in the top of the ch-3, do not turn.

RND 2: Ch 3, *ch 2, (3 dc, ch 2, 3 dc) in next ch sp; rep from * 4 times, ch 2, (3 dc, ch 2, 2 dc) in next ch sp, sl st in top of ch-3, do not turn.

RND 3: Ch 3, 2 dc in ch-2 sp, ch 2, (3 dc, ch 2, 3 dc) in next ch-2 sp, *ch 2, 3 dc in next ch-2 sp, ch 2, (3 dc, ch 2, 3 dc) in corner ch-2 sp; rep from * 4 times, ch 2, sl st in top of ch-3 sp.

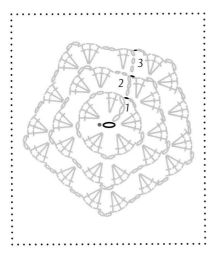

91 Pointed Petal Flower

Foundation: Ch 1, do not turn.

RND 1: Ch 4, then work foll sts in the 5th ch from the hk; dc, *ch 1, dc; rep from * 8 times, ch 1, sl st in the top of the ch-4, do not turn.

RND 2: Ch 3, 3 dc in ch-1 sp, *ch 1, dc in next ch-1 sp, ch 1, 4 dc in next ch-1 sp; rep from * 4 times, ch 1, dc in next ch-1 sp, ch 1, sl st in top of ch-3, do not turn.

RND 3: Ch 5, sc in ch-1 sp, *ch 3, sc in ch-1 sp, ch 5, sc in ch-1 sp; rep from * 4 times, ch 3, sc in next ch-1 sp, do not turn.

RND 4: Ch 3, (4 dc, ch 3, 5 dc) in ch-5 sp, sc in ch-3 sp, *(5 dc, ch 3, 5 dc) in ch-5 sp, sc in ch-3 sp; rep from * 4 times, sl st to top of ch-3.

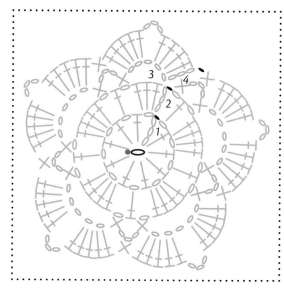

92 Rounded Petal Flower

Foundation: Ch 4, do not turn.

RND 1: 11 dc in the 4th ch from the hk, sl st in the top of ch-4, do not turn.

RND 2: Ch 4, dc, *ch 2, dc; rep from * 10 times, ch 2, sl st in ch-4, do not turn.

RND 3: Ch 3, dc in ch-4 sp, *ch 2, 2 dc in ch-2 sp; rep from * 11 times, ch 2, sl st in top of ch-3, do not turn.

RND 4: Sc in first dc, *ch 5, sc in next dc pair; rep from * 11 times, ch 5, sl st in first sc of row, do not turn.

RND 5: Sl st in first 2 ch of ch-5 sp, sc in center of same ch-5 sp, *9 dc in next ch-5 sp, sc in next ch-5 sp; rep from * 6 times, ending with a sl st in the first sc instead of a sc in the next ch-5 sp.

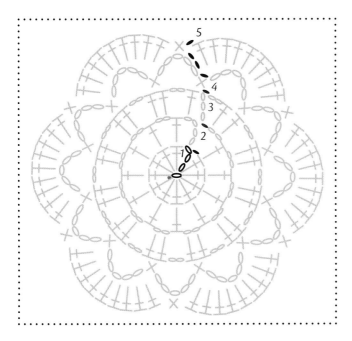

93 Spiral

Foundation: Ch 4, do not turn.

RND 1: 11 dc in the 4th ch from the hk, sl st in the top of the ch-4, do not turn.

RND 2: *Ch 3, sk 1, sc; rep from * 6 times, do not turn.

RND 3: *2 sc in ch-3 sp, ch 3; rep from * 6 times, ending with ch 4 instead of ch 3, do not turn.

RND 4: *(Sc in sc) twice, sc in ch-3 sp, ch 4; rep from * 6 times, do not turn.

RND 5: *(Sc in sc) 3 times, 2 sc in ch-3 sp, ch 4; rep from * 6 times, do not turn.

RND 6: *(Sc in sc) 5 times, 2 sc in ch-3 sp, ch 4; rep from * 6 times, do not turn.

RND 7: *Sk 1, (sc in sc) 6 times, 2 sc in ch-3 sp, ch 4; rep from * 6 times, do not turn.

RND 8: *Sk 1, (sc in sc) 7 times, 2 sc in ch-3 sp, ch 4; rep from * 6 times, do not turn.

RND 9: *Sk 1, (sc in sc) 8 times, 2 sc in ch-3 sp, ch 4; rep from * 6 times, ending with sl st in the next ch sp instead of ch 4.

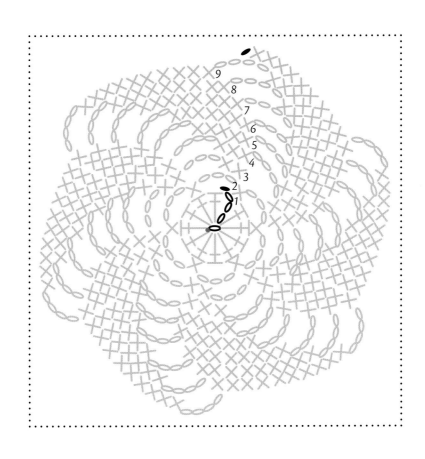

94 Frilly Flower

Foundation: Ch 4, do not turn.

RND 1: 11 dc in the 4th ch from hk, sl st in the top of ch-4, do not turn.

RND 2: Ch 1, sc in 1st st, 2 sc in ea st around, sl st in ch-1, do not turn.

RND 3: Ch 4, sk sl st and 1st sc, sc, *ch 3, sk 2, sc; rep from * 6 times, ch 3, sc in sl st, do not turn.

RND 4: Sl st in ch-4 sp, sc in same ch-4 sp, *ch 7, sc in next ch-3 sp; rep from * 7 times, ch 7, sc in top of sc at beg of row, do not turn.

RND 5: (Ch 3, sc in ch-7 sp) 4 times, *ch 1, sc in next ch-7 sp, (ch 3, sc) in same ch-7 sp 3 times; rep from * 7 times, sl st in ch 3 at beg of row.

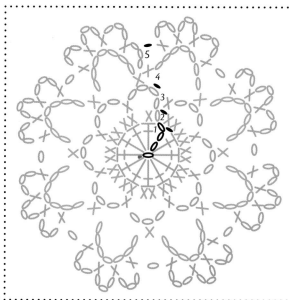

Color Changing Rows

95 Mini Color Blocks

Multiple of 4 stitches, plus 3

Shown with 3 colors (A, B and C). Work the Foundation and Row 1 with Yarn A, then change the yarn at the beginning of each new row, alternating between Yarns A, B and C.

Foundation: Ch a multiple of 4 sts, plus 3, turn.

ROW 1: Ch 3, sc in 6th ch from hk, sc, *ch 2, sk 2, 2 sc; rep from * to last 3 ch, ch 2, sk 2, sc, turn.

ROW 2: Ch 1, 2 sc in ch-2 sp, *ch 2, 2 sc in next ch-2 sp; rep from * across, turn.

ROW 3: Ch 3, 2 sc in ch-2 sp, *ch 2, 2 sc in next ch-2 sp; rep from * across, ch 2, sc in ch sp at end of row, turn.

Rep Rows 2–3 to cont patt.

96 Green Waves

Multiple of 8 stitches, plus 5

Shown with 2 colors (A and B). Work the Foundation and Row 1 with Yarn A, then change the yarn at the beginning of each new row, alternating between Yarns A and B.

Foundation: Ch a multiple of 8 sts, plus 5, turn.

ROW 1: Ch 1, sc in 2nd ch from hk and ea ch across, turn.

ROW 2: Ch 1, 3 sc, *hdc, 3 dc, hdc, 3 sc; rep from * to last 2 sts, hdc, dc, turn.

ROWS 3 AND 5: Ch 1, sc in ea st across, turn.

ROW 4: Ch 3, 3 dc, hdc, *3 sc, hdc, 3 dc, hdc; rep from * to last st, sc, turn.

Rep Rows 2-5 to cont patt.

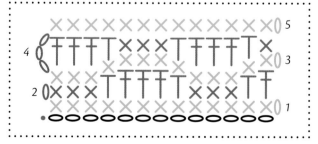

97 Stretched Stitch Stripes

Multiple of 4 stitches, plus 1
Shown with 3 colors (A, B and C)

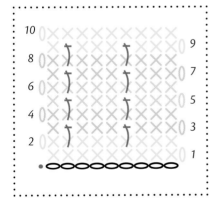

Foundation: With A, ch a multiple of 4 sts, plus 1, turn.

ROW 1: With A, ch 1, sc in the 2nd ch from hk and ea ch across, turn.

ROW 2: Ch 1, sc in ea st across, turn.

ROW 3: With B, ch 1, *3 sc, sc in row below; rep from * to last st, sc, turn.

ROW 4: Rep Row 2 with B.

ROW 5: Rep Row 3 with C.

ROW 6: Rep Row 2 with C.

ROW 7: Rep Row 3 with B.

ROW 8: Rep Row 2 with B.

ROW 9: Rep Row 3 with A.

ROW 10: Rep Row 2 with A.

Rep Rows 3–10 to cont patt.

98 Hanging Flowers

Multiple of 5 stitches, plus 4
Shown with 2 colors (A and B)

Foundation: With A, ch a multiple of 5 sts, plus 4, turn.

ROW 1: With A, ch 1, sc in the 2nd ch from hk and ea ch across, turn.

ROWS 2, 3, 4 AND 6: Ch 1, sc in ea st across, turn.

ROW 5: With B, ch 1, *4 sc, make a 3-dc cluster; work the first st 2 rows below and back 1 st, the second st directly down 3 rows and the third st 2 rows below and forward 1 st; rep from * to last 4 sts, 4 sc, turn.

Rep Rows 2–6 to cont patt.

99 Post Checker Stripes

Multiple of 3 stitches, plus 1
Shown with 2 colors (A and B)

Foundation: With A, ch a multiple of 3 sts, plus 1, turn.

ROW 1: With A, ch 1, sc in 2nd ch from hk and ea ch across, turn.

ROW 2: Ch 1, sc in ea st across, turn.

ROW 3: With B, ch 1, *2 sc, FPdc; rep from * to last st, sc, turn.

ROW 4: Ch 1, sc in ea st across, turn.

ROW 5: With A, ch 1, *2 sc, FPdc; rep from * to last st, sc, turn.

ROW 6: Ch, 1, sc in ea st across, turn.

Rep Rows 3–6 to cont patt.

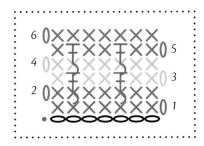

Colorwork

100 Double Crochet Checkerboard

Multiple of 6 stitches, plus 2, worked in the round

Shown with 2 colors (A and B)

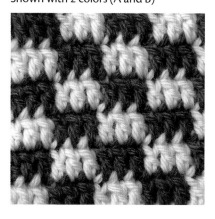

Foundation: With A, ch a multiple of 6 sts, plus 2, join into a circle with a sl st, do not turn.

RND 1: Ch 1, sc in 2nd ch from hk and ea ch across, sl st in the ch-1.

RND 2: With A, ch 3, 2 dc, *3 dc in B, 3 dc in A; rep from * around, sl st in top of ch-3, do not turn.

RND 3: With B, ch 3, 2 dc, *3 dc in A, 3 dc in B; rep from * around, sl st in top of ch-3, do not turn.

Rep Rnds 2–3 to cont patt.

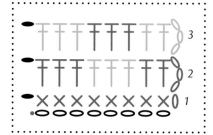

101 Colorwork Dots

Multiple of 2 stitches, plus 1, worked in
the round
Shown with 2 colors (A and B)

Foundation: With A, ch a multiple of 2
sts, plus 1, join into a circle with a sl st,
do not turn.

RND 1: Ch 1, sc in 2nd ch from hk and ea
ch across, sl st in the ch-1.

RND 2: With A, ch 1, sc, *sc in B, sc in A;
rep from * around, sl st in top of ch-1, do
not turn.

RND 3: With A, ch 1, sc in ea st across, sl
st in the ch-1, do not turn.

Rep Rnds 2–3 to cont patt.

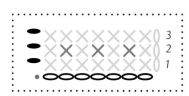

102 Colorwork Spots

Multiple of 10 stitches, worked
in the round
Shown with 2 colors (A and B)

Foundation: With A, ch a multiple of 10
sts, join into a circle with a sl st, do not
turn.

RND 1: Ch 1, sc in 2nd ch from hk and ea
ch around, sl st in the ch-1.

RNDS 2 AND 6: With A, ch 1, 6 sc, *3 sc
in B, 7 sc in A; rep from * around, ending
with 1 sc in A instead of 7 sc, sl st in top
of ch-1, do not turn.

RNDS 3, 4 AND 5: With A ch 1, *5 sc in A,
5 sc in B; rep from * around, sl st in top of
ch-1, do not turn.

RNDS 7, 8, 9, 15, 16 AND 17: With A, ch
1, sc in ea st around, sl st in the ch-1, do
not turn.

RNDS 10 AND 14: With A, ch 1, sc, *3 sc
in B, 7 sc in A; rep from * around, ending
with 6 sc in A instead of 7 sc, sl st in top
of ch-1, do not turn.

RNDS 11, 12 AND 13: With B, ch 1, *5 sc
in B, 5 sc in A; rep from * around, sl st in
top of ch-1, do not turn.

Rep Rnds 2–17 to cont patt.

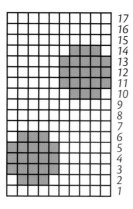

17
16
15
14
13
12
11
10
9
8
7
6
5
4
3
2
1

103 Colorwork Triangles

Multiple of 12 stitches, plus 6, worked in the round

Shown with 4 colors (A, B, C and D)

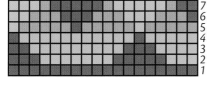

Foundation: With A, ch a multiple of 12 sts, plus 6, join into a circle with a sl st, do not turn.

RND 1: Ch 1, sc in 2nd ch from hk and ea ch around, sl st in the ch-1.

RND 2: With B, ch 1, 2 sc, *1 sc in C, 5 sc in A, 1 sc in C, 5 sc in B; rep from * to last 4 sts, 1 sc in C, 3 sc in A, sl st in ch-1, do not turn.

RND 3: With B, ch 1, 1 sc, *3 sc in C, 3 sc in A, 3 sc in C, 3 sc in B; rep from * to last 5 sts, 3 sc in C, 2 sc in A, sl st in ch-1, do not turn.

RND 4: With C, ch 1, *5 sc in C, 1 sc in A, 5 sc in C, 1 sc in B; rep from * to last 6 sts, 5 sc in C, 1 sc in A, sl st in ch-1, do not turn.

RND 5: With D, ch 1, *5 sc in D, 1 sc in B, 5 sc in D, 1 sc in A; rep from * to last 6 sts, 5 sc in D, 1 sc in B, sl st in ch-1, do not turn.

RND 6: With A, ch 1, 1 sc, *3 sc in D, 3 sc in B, 3 sc in D, 3 sc in A; rep from * to last 5 sts, 3 sc in D, 2 sc in B, sl st in ch-1, do not turn.

RND 7: With A, ch 1, 2 sc, *1 sc in D, 5 sc in B, 1 sc in D, 5 sc in A; rep from * to last 4 sts, 1 sc in D, 3 sc in B, sl st in ch-1, do not turn.

Rep Rnds 2–7 to cont patt.

Bead Crochet

104 Scattered Beads

Multiple of 4 stitches, plus 5

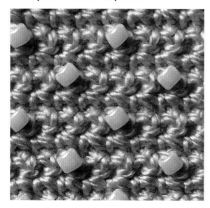

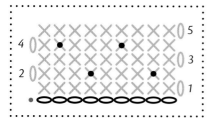

To calculate how many beads you will need: multiply the number of repeats of the pattern by 2 and add 1; divide the number of rows by 4; multiply the two previous calculations together. Example: for a 3 repeat by 12 row swatch: $(3 \times 2) + 1 = 7$; $12 \div 4 = 3$; $7 \times 3 = 21$ beads.

String the beads on the yarn or thread.

Foundation: Ch a multiple of 4 sts, plus 5, turn.

ROW 1: Ch 1, sc in 2nd ch from hk and ea ch across, turn.

ROW 2: Ch 1, *3 sc, scB; rep from * to last st, sc, turn.

ROWS 3 AND 5: Ch 1, sc in ea st across, turn.

ROW 4: Ch 1, sc, *scB, 3 sc; rep from * across, turn.

Rep Rows 2–5 to cont patt.

105 Bead Drapes and Dots

Multiple of 3 stitches

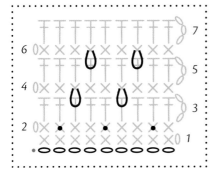

Special Stitch ⋃

sc5B - single crochet, sliding 5 beads down to the hook so the loop of 5 beads is encased in the stitch as you make the stitch.

To calculate how many beads you will need: multiply the number of repeats of the pattern by 11 and add 1; divide the number of rows by 6; multiply the two previous calculations together. Example: for a 3 repeat by 12 row swatch: $(3 \times 11) + 1 = 34$; $12 \div 6 = 2$; $34 \times 2 = 68$ beads. String the beads on the yarn or thread.

Foundation: Ch a multiple of 3 sts, turn.

ROW 1: Ch 1, sc in 2nd ch from hk and ea ch across, turn.

ROW 2: Ch 1, sc, scB, *2 sc, scB; rep from * to last st, sc, turn.

ROWS 3, 5 AND 7: Ch 3, dc in ea st across, turn.

ROW 4: Ch 1, *2 sc, sc5B; rep from * to last 3 sts, 3 sc, turn.

ROW 6: Ch 1, 3 sc, sc5B, *2 sc, sc5B; rep from * to last 2 sts, 2 sc, turn.

Rep Rows 2–7 to cont patt.

106 Bead Lace

Multiple of 8 stitches, plus 3; pattern
begins with a multiple of 6 sts, plus 1

To calculate how many beads you will
need: multiply the number of repeats
of the pattern by 2; divide the number
of rows by 4; multiply the two previous
calculations together. Example: for a 3
repeat by 12 row swatch: (3 × 2) = 6; 12
÷ 4 = 3; 6 × 3 = 18 beads.

String the beads on the yarn or thread.

Foundation: Ch a multiple of 6 sts, plus
1, turn.

ROW 1: Ch 3, (dc, ch 1, dc) in 4th ch
from hk, *ch 1, sk 2 ch, (dc, ch 1, dc) in
next ch; rep from * across, turn.

ROW 2: Ch 3, (dc, ch 1, dc) in ch-1 sp, *ch
1, sk ch-1 sp, (dc, ch 1, dc) in next ch-1
sp, chB, sk ch-1 sp, (dc, ch 1, dc) in next
ch-1 sp; rep from * across, turn.

ROWS 3 AND 5: Ch 3, (dc, ch 1, dc) in
ch-1 sp, *ch 1, sk ch-1 sp, (dc, ch 1, dc) in
next ch-1 sp; rep from * across, turn.

ROW 4: Ch 3, *(dc, ch 1, dc) in ch-1 sp,
chB, sk ch-1 sp, (dc, ch 1, dc) in next ch-1
sp, ch 1, sk ch-1 sp; rep from * to last ch-1
sp, (dc, ch 1, dc) in last ch-1 sp, turn.

Rep Rows 2–5 to cont patt.

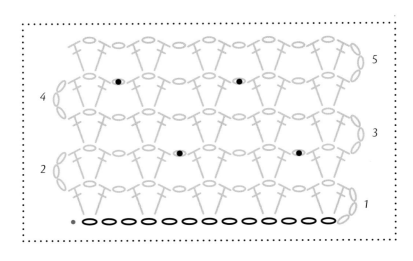

107 Beaded Shells

Multiple of 7 stitches

To calculate how many beads you will need: multiply the number of repeats of the pattern by 17.

String the beads on the yarn or thread.

Foundation: Ch a multiple of 7 sts, turn.

Special Stitch

dcB = slide one bead down to the hook, make a double crochet, encasing the bead into the stitch as you make the stitch.

ROW 1: Ch 3, dc in 4th ch from hk and ea ch across, turn.

ROW 2: Ch 1, scB in ea st across, turn.

ROW 3: Ch 3, dc in ea st across, turn.

ROW 4: Ch 1, *scB, sk 2 dc, 9 dcB in next st, sk 2 dc, sc in next dc; rep from * across.

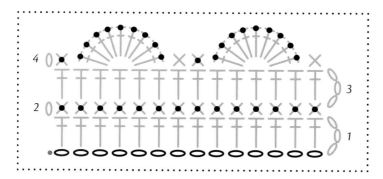

108 Bead Heart

This pattern is worked in the round. The beaded portion of the pattern covers 9 stitches; add additional stitches to form a tube.

String 38 beads on the yarn or thread.

Foundation: Ch 9, plus the desired number of sts for the remainder of the tube, do not turn.

RND 1: 4 sc, scB, 4 sc.

RND 2: 3 sc, 3 scB, 3 sc.

RND 3: 2 sc, 5 scB, 2 sc.

RND 4: Sc, 7 scB, sc.

RNDS 5 AND 6: 9 scB.

RND 7: Sc, 2 scB, 3 sc, 2 scB, sc.

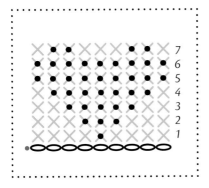

109 Bead Star

Note: This pattern is worked in a spiral in 6 equal sections. Only 1 section is pictured in the chart.

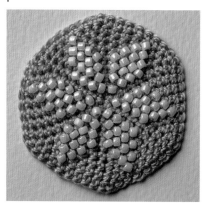

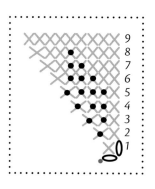

String 96 beads on the yarn or thread.

Foundation: Ch 2, do not turn.

RND 1: 6 sc in 2nd ch from hk, do not turn—6 sts.

RND 2: (Sc, scB) in ea st around—12 sts.

RND 3: *Sc, (2 scB) in next st; rep from * around—18 sts.

RND 4: *Sc, scB, (2 scB) in next st; rep from * around—24 sts.

RND 5: *Sc, 2 scB, (2 scB) in next st; rep from * around—30 sts.

RND 6: *2 sc, 2 scB, (scB, sc) in next st; rep from * around—36 sts.

RND 7: *3 sc, 2 scB, (2 sc) in next st; rep from * around—42 sts.

RND 8: *4 sc, scB, sc, (2 sc) in next st; rep from * around—48 sts.

RND 9: *7 sc, (2 sc) in next st; rep from * around—54 sts.

110 Bead Cord

This pattern is worked counterclockwise from the inside of the tube.

Shown with 6 bead colors.

Special Stitch

Bsl st = slide a bead down to the hook then make a slip stitch, encasing the bead into the slip stitch as you make the stitch.

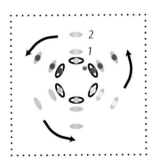

To calculate how many beads you will need: multiply the number of rounds by 6.

String the beads on the yarn or thread, one bead of each color in the same order for each round.

Foundation: 6 chB, do not join.

RND 1: Bsl st in 6th chB from hk and ea chB around, do not turn.

RND 2: Bsl st in each st around, do not turn.

Rep Rnd 2 to cont patt.

Edgings and Insertions

111 Basic Loop Edging

Multiple of 4 stitches, plus 1

Foundation: Ch a multiple of 4 sts, plus 1, turn.

ROW 1: Ch 3, dc in 4th ch from hk and ea ch across, turn.

ROW 2: Ch 1, sc, *ch 5, sk 3, sc; rep from * across.

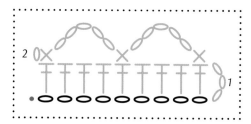

112 Double Loops

Multiple of 6 stitches, plus 1

Foundation: Ch a multiple of 6 sts, plus 1, turn.

ROW 1: Ch 3, dc in 4th ch from hk and ea ch across, turn.

ROW 2: Ch 1, 2 sc, *ch 5, sk 3, 3 sc; rep from * across, ending with 2 sc instead of 3 sc, turn.

ROW 3: *Ch 9, sl st in center sc of 3 sc set; rep from * across, ending with sl st in last sc of row.

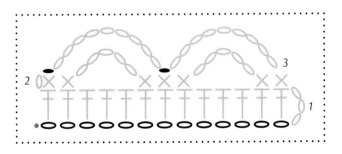

113 Simple Picot

Multiple of 3 stitches, plus 1

Foundation: Ch a multiple of 3 sts, plus 1, turn.

ROW 1: Ch 3, dc in 4th ch from hk and ea ch across, turn.

ROW 2: Ch 1, 2 sc, *ch 5, 3 sc; rep from * across, ending with 2 sc instead of 3 sc.

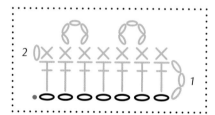

114 Loop

Multiple of 5 stitches, plus 1

Foundation: Ch a multiple of 5 sts, plus 1, turn.

ROW 1: Ch 3, dc in 4th ch from hk and ea ch across, turn.

ROW 2: Ch 1, sc, *ch 5, sk 2, sc, ch 1, sk 1, sc; rep from * across.

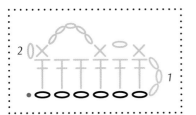

115 Picot and Loop

Multiple of 3 stitches, plus 1

Foundation: Ch a multiple of 3 sts, plus 1, turn.

ROW 1: Ch 3, dc in 4th ch from hk and ea ch across, turn.

ROW 2: Ch 1, sc, *ch 5, sk 2, (sc, ch 3, sc) in next st; rep from * across.

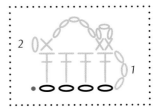

116 Small Shells

Multiple of 3 stitches

Foundation: Ch a multiple of 3 sts, turn.
ROW 1: Ch 3, dc in 4th ch from hk and ea ch across, turn.
ROW 2: Ch 3, sk 1, 3 dc in next st, *sk 2, 3 dc in next st; rep from * to end, dc in ch sp at end of row.

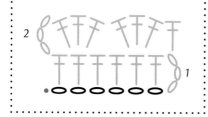

117 Shells and Loops

Multiple of 3 stitches

Foundation: Ch a multiple of 3 sts, turn.

ROW 1: Ch 3, dc in 4th ch from hk and ea ch across, turn.

ROW 2: Ch 3, sk 1, 3 dc in next st, *sk 2, 3 dc in next st; rep from * to end, dc in ch sp at end of row, turn.

ROW 3: Ch 1, sc in 2nd dc of 3-dc shell, *ch 5, sc in 2nd dc of next 3-dc shell; rep from * across.

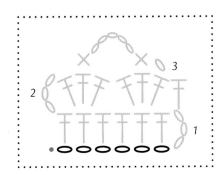

118 Scallops

Multiple of 6 stitches

Foundation: Ch a multiple of 6 sts, turn.

ROW 1: Ch 3, dc in 4th ch from hk and ea ch across, turn.

ROW 2: *Sk 2, 6 dc in next st, sk 2, sc in next st; rep from * across.

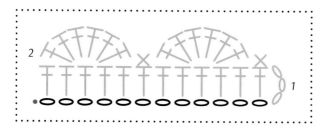

119 Shells and Picots

Multiple of 8 stitches, plus 7

Foundation: Ch a multiple of 8 sts, plus 7, turn.

ROW 1: Ch 3, dc in 4th ch from hk and ea ch across, turn.

ROW 2: Ch 4, sk 1, 3 dc, *ch 1, sk 1, 3 dc; rep from * across, ending with 2 dc instead of 3 dc, turn.

ROW 3: Ch 3, *(3 dc, ch 7, sl st in 6th ch from hk, ch 1, 3 dc) in ch-1 sp, ch 1, dc in next ch-1 sp, ch 1; rep from * across, ending with dc instead of ch 1.

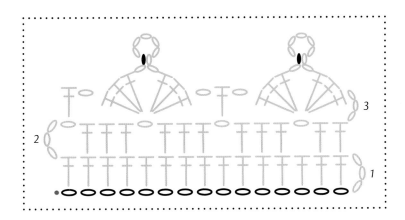

120 Open Arches

Multiple of 6 stitches, plus 1

Foundation: Ch a multiple of 6 sts, plus 1, turn.

ROW 1: Ch 3, dc in 4th ch from hk and ea ch across, turn.

ROW 2: Ch 1, 2 sc, *ch 5, sk 3, 3 sc; rep from * across, ending with 2 sc instead of 3 sc, turn.

ROW 3: Ch 1, *10 dc in ch-5 sp; rep from * across, sc in last st.

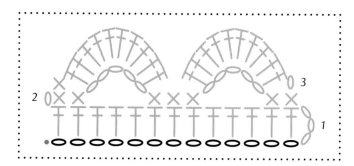

121 Rick Rack

Multiple of 10 stitches, plus 1

Foundation: Ch a multiple of 10 sts, plus 1, turn.

ROW 1: Ch 3, dc in 4th ch from hk and ea ch across, turn.

ROW 2: Ch 1, sc, *ch 13, sk 9, sc; rep from * across, turn.

ROW 3: Ch 3, *sk 1 ch, 4 dc, 2 dc in next ch, ch 3, sk 1, 2 dc in next ch, 4 dc, sk 1 ch, sk sc; rep from * across, dc in ch sp at end of row, turn.

ROW 4: Ch 3, sk 2 dc, *4 dc, (2 dc, ch 3, 2 dc) in ch-3, 4 dc, sk 4 dc; rep from * across, ending with sk 2 dc, dc in ch sp at end of row, turn.

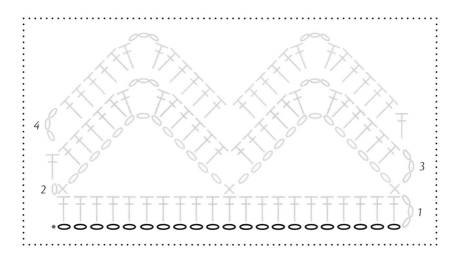

122 Picots and Halos

Multiple of 8 stitches, plus 5

Foundation: Ch a multiple of 8 sts, plus 5, turn.

ROW 1: Ch 3, dc in 4th ch from hk and ea ch across, turn.

ROW 2: Ch 1, sc, *ch 4, sk 3, sc; rep from * across, turn.

ROW 3: Ch 3, 7 dc in ch-4 sp, *sc in next ch-4 sp, 7 dc in next ch-4 sp; rep from * across, turn.

ROW 4: Ch 4, (sc, ch 3, sc) in 4th dc of 7-dc shell, *ch 3 (sc, ch 3, sc) in sc between shells, ch 3, (sc, ch3, sc) in 4th dc of 7-dc shell; rep from * across, ch 3, sc in ch sp at end of row, turn.

ROW 5: Sl st in first 2 ch of ch-3 sp, sc in ch-3 sp, *ch 5, sc in next ch-3 sp; rep from * across, ending with sc in ch sp at end of row.

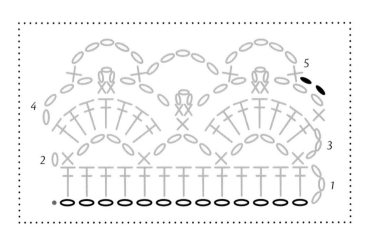

123 Vertical Shells Inset

Foundation: Ch 1, turn.

ROW 1: Ch 3, (2 dc, ch 2, 3 dc) in 4th ch from hk, turn.

ROW 2: Ch 3, (3 dc, ch 2, 3 dc) in ch-2 sp, dc in ch sp at end of row, turn.

Rep Row 2 to cont patt.

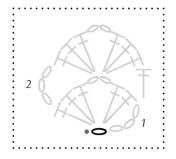

124 Ribbon Casing

Multiple of 2 stitches

Foundation: Ch a multiple of 2 sts, turn.

ROW 1: Ch 1, sc in 2nd ch from hk and ea ch across, turn.

ROW 2: Ch 4, sk 1, dc, *ch 1, sk 1, dc; rep from * across, turn.

ROW 3: Ch 1, sc in ea st and ch across.

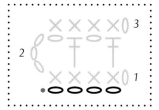

125 Vertical shells with border

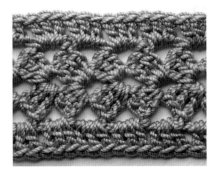

Foundation: Ch 1, turn.

ROW 1: Ch 3, (2 dc, ch 2, 3 dc) in 4th ch from hk, turn.

ROW 2: Ch 3, (3 dc, ch 2, 3 dc) in ch-2 sp, dc in ch sp at end of row, turn.

ROW 3: Ch 3, (3 dc, ch 2, 3 dc) in ch-2 sp, dc in ch sp at end of row, turn.

Rep Row 3 to cont patt, making the strip of edging as long as you choose.

When the strip is the length you want, work the following row around the perimeter:

NEXT ROW: Ch 3, 2 dc in dc at end of row, *ch 1, 3 dc in next ch sp or dc along side of strip; rep from * along the side to last ch sp. Ch 1, work 5 dc in last ch sp or dc on side, ch 1, work 5 dc in the foundation ch, ch 1, work 5 dc in the first ch sp or dc at the beg of the other side of the strip. **Ch 1, 3 dc in next ch sp or dc; rep from ** along remaining side of the strip to the last ch sp or dc on the side of the strip. Work 5 dc in the last ch sp or dc at the end of the strip. Ch 1, 5 dc in the ch-2 sp at the end of the strip, ch 1, 2 dc in same space as ch 3 and 2 dc at beg of row. Join to the top of the ch-3 at the beg of row with a sl st.

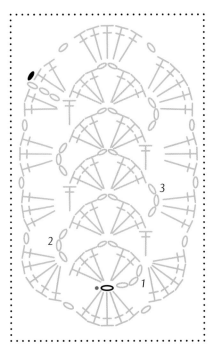

126 Scalloped Ribbon Casing

Multiple of 4 stitches, plus 2

Foundation: Ch a multiple of 4 sts, plus 2, turn.

ROW 1: Ch 1, sc in 2nd ch from hk and ea ch across, turn.

ROW 2: Ch 4, sk 1, dc, * ch 1, sk 1, dc; rep from * across, turn.

ROW 3: Ch 1, sc in ea st and ch across, turn.

ROW 4: Ch 3, 4 dc in 1st st, *sk 3, 5 dc in next st; rep from * to last st, hdc in ch sp at end of row.

NEXT ROW: Attach a new length of yarn or thread to the Foundation ch and rep Row 4 on the opposite side.

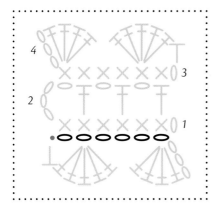

Lace Backgrounds

127 Basic Loop Net

Multiple of 4 stitches, plus 3

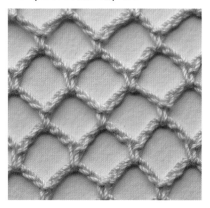

Foundation: Ch a multiple of 4 sts, plus 3, turn.

ROW 1: Ch 5, sc in 8th ch from hk, *ch 5, sk 3 ch, sc in next ch; rep from * across, turn.

ROW 2: *Ch 5, sc in ch-5 sp; rep from * across, ending with sc in ch sp at end of row, turn.

Rep Row 2 to cont patt.

LAST ROW: Ch 5, sc in ch-5 sp, *ch 3, sc in next ch-5; rep from * across, ending with ch 4, sc in ch sp at end of row.

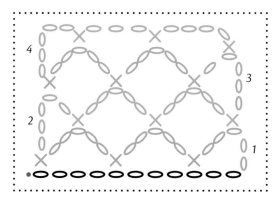

128 Picot Loop Net

Multiple of 5 stitches

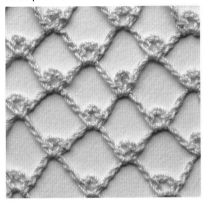

Foundation: Ch a multiple of 5 sts, turn.

ROW 1: Ch 7, sc in 11th ch from hk, ch 4, sc in next ch, *ch 7, sk 3, sc, ch 4, sc; rep from * across, turn.

ROW 2: *Ch 7, (sc, ch 4, sc) in ch-7 sp; rep from * across, turn.

Rep Row 2 to cont patt.

LAST ROW: Ch 6, sc in ch-7 sp, *ch 4, sc in next ch-7 sp; rep from * across.

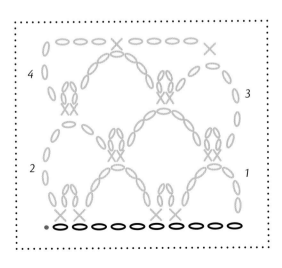

129 Double Crochet Net

Multiple of 4 stitches

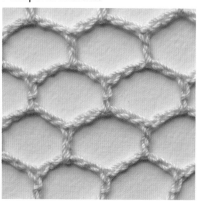

Foundation: Ch a multiple of 4 sts, turn.

ROW 1: Ch 6, dc in 10th ch from hk, *ch 5, sk 3, dc in next ch; rep from * across, turn.

ROW 2: Ch 6, dc in ch-5 sp, *ch 5, dc in ch-5 sp; rep from * across, ch 5, dc in ch sp at end of row, turn.

Rep Row 2 to cont patt.

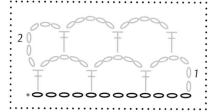

130 V-Stitch Net

Multiple of 6 stitches, plus 4

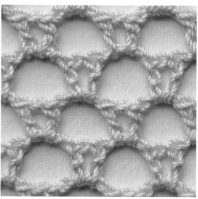

Foundation: Ch a multiple of 6 sts, plus 4, turn.

ROW 1: Ch 5, (dc, ch 1, dc) in 9th ch from hk, *ch 3, sk 5, (dc, ch 1, dc) in next ch; rep from * across, turn.

ROW 2: Ch 5, (dc, ch 1, dc) in ch-3 sp, *ch 3, (dc, ch 1, dc) in next ch sp; rep from * across, ch 3, (dc, ch 1, dc) in ch sp at end of row, turn.

Rep Row 2 to cont patt.

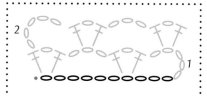

Filet

131 Filet ZigZag Border

Multiple of 8 stitches, plus 1

Foundation: Ch a multiple of 8 sts, plus 1, turn.

ROW 1: Ch 4, dc in 6th ch from hk, ch 1, sk 1 ch, dc, ch 1, sk 1 ch, 3 dc, *(ch 1, sk 1 ch, dc) twice, ch 1, sk 1 ch, 3 dc; rep from * across, turn.

ROW 2: Ch 3, *ch 1, sk 1 dc, dc in dc, dc in ch, dc in dc, ch 1, sk 1 ch, dc in dc, dc in ch, dc in dc; rep from * across, ending with dc in top of ch sp at end of row, turn.

ROW 3: Ch 4, sk 1 dc, dc in dc, dc in ch, dc in dc, *ch 1, sk 1 dc, dc in dc, ch 1, sk 1 ch, dc in dc, ch 1, sk 1 dc, dc in dc, dc in ch, dc in dc; rep from * to last 2 squares, ch 1, sk 1 dc, dc in dc, ch 1, sk 1 ch, dc in top of ch sp at end of row, turn.

ROW 4: Ch 4, sk 1 ch, dc in dc, ch 1, sk 1 ch, (dc in dc) 3 times, *(ch 1, sk ch, dc in dc) 3 times, 2 dc; rep to last square, ch 1, sk 1 ch, dc in top of ch sp at end of row, turn.

ROW 5: Ch 3, *ch 1, sk ch or dc, dc in dc; rep from * across, ending with dc in top of ch sp at end of row, turn.

ROW 6: Ch 3, *ch 1, sk ch, dc in dc; rep from * across, ending with dc in ch sp at end of row, turn.

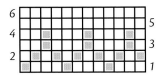

132 Filet Diamond Motif

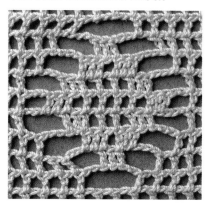

Foundation: Ch 31, turn.

ROW 1: Ch 4, dc in 6th ch from hk, *ch 1, sk 1, dc; rep from * across, turn.

ROW 2: Ch 3, (ch 1, sk ch, dc in dc) 6 times, ch 5, sk 5 ch or dc, dc in dc, (ch 1, sk ch, dc in dc) 5 times, ch 1, sk ch, dc in 3rd ch of ch sp at end of row, turn.

ROW 3: Ch 3, (ch 1, sk ch, dc in dc) 5 times, ch 4, sk (ch, dc and 1st ch of ch-5 sp), dc in next 3 dc, ch 4, sk (last ch of ch-5 sp, dc and ch), dc in dc, (ch 1, sk ch, dc in dc) 5 times, turn.

ROW 4: Ch 3, (ch 1, sk ch, dc in dc) 4 times, ch 4, sk (ch, dc and 1st and 2nd ch of ch-4 sp), dc in 3rd and 4th ch of ch-4 sp, dc in dc, sk 1 dc, dc in next dc, dc in 1st and 2nd ch of next ch-4 sp, ch 4, sk (last 2 ch of ch-4 sp, dc and ch), dc in dc, (ch 1, sk ch, dc in dc) 3 times, ch 1, dc in ch sp at end of row, turn.

ROW 5: Ch 3, (ch 1, sk ch, dc in dc) 3 times, ch 4, sk (ch, dc and 1st and 2nd ch of ch-4 sp) dc in 3rd and 4th ch of ch-4 sp, dc in dc, ch 1, sk dc, dc in next dc, ch 1, sk ch, dc in dc, ch 1, sk dc, dc in next dc, dc in 1st and 2nd ch of ch-4 sp, ch

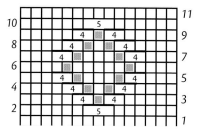

4, sk (3rd and 4th ch of ch-4 sp, dc and ch), dc in next dc, (ch 1, sk ch, dc in dc) twice, ch 1, dc in top of ch sp at end of row, turn.

ROW 6: Ch 3, (ch 1, sk ch, dc in dc) 3 times, ch 1, sk 1st and 2nd ch of ch-4 sp, dc in 3rd and 4th ch of ch-4 sp, dc in dc, ch 1, sk dc, dc in next dc, (ch 1, sk ch, dc in dc) 3 times, ch 1, sk dc, dc in next dc, dc in 1st and 2nd ch of ch-4 sp, ch 1, sk 3rd and 4th ch of ch-4 sp, dc in next dc, (ch 1, sk ch, dc in dc) twice, ch 1, dc in top of ch sp at end of row, turn.

ROW 7: Ch 3, (ch 1, sk ch, dc in dc) 3 times, ch 4, sk ch and 2 dc, dc in next dc, dc in ch, dc in dc, (ch 1, sk ch, dc in next dc) 3 times, dc in ch, dc in dc, ch 4, sk 2 dc and ch, dc in next dc, (ch 1, sk ch, dc in dc) twice, ch 1, dc in top of ch sp at end of row, turn.

ROW 8: Ch 3, (ch 1, sk ch, dc in dc) 3 times, ch 1, sk 1st ch in ch-4 sp, dc in 2nd ch of ch-4 sp, ch 4, sk (1st and 2nd ch of ch-4 sp and 2 dc), dc in next dc, dc in ch, dc in dc, ch 1, sk ch, dc in next dc, dc in ch, dc in dc, ch 4, sk (2 dc and 1st and

2nd ch of ch-4 sp), dc in 3rd ch of ch-4 sp, (ch 1, sk ch, dc in dc) 3 times, ch 1, dc in top of ch sp at end of row, turn.

ROW 9: Ch 3, (ch 1, sk ch, dc in dc) 4 times, ch 1, sk 1st ch in ch-4 sp, dc in 2nd ch of ch-4 sp, ch 4, sk (1st and 2nd ch of ch-4 and 2 dc), dc in next dc, dc in ch, dc in dc, ch 4, sk (2 dc and 1st and 2nd ch of ch-4 sp), dc in 3rd ch of ch-4, (ch 1, sk ch, dc in dc) 4 times, ch 1, dc in top of ch sp at end of row, turn.

ROW 10: Ch 3, (ch 1, sk ch, dc in dc) 5 times, ch 1, sk 1st ch in ch-4 sp, dc in 2nd ch of ch-4 sp, ch 5, sk (3rd and 4th ch of ch-4 sp, 3 dc, and 1st and 2nd ch of next ch-4 sp), dc in 3rd ch of ch-4 sp, (ch 1, sk ch, dc in dc) 5 times, ch 1, dc in top of ch sp at end of row, turn.

ROW 11: Ch 3, *ch 1, sk ch, dc in next dc or ch; rep from * across.

133 Filet Draped Border

Multiple of 16 stitches, plus 1

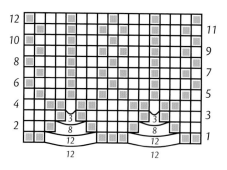

Foundation: Ch a multiple of 16 sts, plus 1, turn.

ROW 1: Ch 3, dc in 4th ch from hk and next 3 ch, *ch 12, sk 12 ch, dc in next 7 ch; rep from * across, ending with dc in next 5 ch instead of next 7 ch, turn.

ROW 2: Ch 3, (ch 1, sk 1, dc) twice, (2 dc, ch 8, 2 dc) in ch-12 sp, dc in dc, *(ch 1, sk 1, dc) 3 times, (2 dc, ch 8, 2 dc) in ch-12 sp, dc in dc; rep from * to last 2 squares, ch 1, sk 1, dc, ch 1, sk 1, dc in top of ch sp at end of row, turn.

ROW 3: Ch 3, (ch 1, sk ch, dc in dc) twice, ch 1, sk 1, dc, (2 dc, ch 3, 2 dc) in ch-8 sp, dc in dc, *(ch 1, sk 1 ch or dc, dc in dc) 5 times, (2 dc, ch 3, 2 dc) in ch-8 sp, dc in dc; rep from * to last 3 squares, ch 1, sk 1, dc, ch 1, sk sp, dc in dc, ch 1, sk ch, dc in top of ch sp at end of row, turn.

ROW 4: Ch 3, (ch 1, sk ch, dc in dc) twice, dc in ch, dc in next 3 dc, ch 1, sk ch-3 sp, dc in next 3 dc, dc in ch, dc in dc, *(ch 1, sk ch, dc in dc) 3 times, dc in ch, dc in next 3 dc, sk ch-3 sp, dc in next 3 dc, dc in dc, dc in dc; rep from * to last 2

squares, ch 1, sk ch, dc in dc, ch 1, sk ch, dc in top of ch-3, turn.

ROW 5: Ch 3, *ch 1, sk ch, dc in dc, dc in ch, dc in dc, (ch 1, sk ch, dc in dc) twice, dc in ch, dc in dc, (ch 1, sk ch, dc in dc) twice, dc in ch, dc in dc, ch 1, sk sp, dc in dc, dc in ch, dc in dc, (ch 1, sk ch, dc in dc) twice, dc in ch, dc in dc; rep from * across, ending with dc in top of ch sp at end of row instead of dc in dc, turn.

ROW 6: Ch 3, dc in ch, dc in dc, *ch 1, sk dc, dc in next dc, (ch 1, sk 1, dc in dc) twice, 2 dc, (ch 1 sk ch, dc in dc) twice, ch 1, sk dc, dc in next dc, dc in ch, dc in dc; rep from * across, turn.

Rep Rows 5–6 to cont the top of the patt.

134 Filet Openwork Border

Multiple of 10 stitches, plus 3

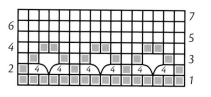

Foundation: Ch a multiple of 10 sts, plus 3, turn.

ROW 1: Ch 3, dc in 4th ch from hk and ea ch across, turn.

ROW 2: Ch 3, 2 dc, *ch 4, sk 3, sc in next st, ch 4, sk 3, 3 dc; rep from * across, working last dc in top of ch sp at end of row, turn.

ROW 3: Ch 3, *ch 1, sk 1, dc in dc, 2 dc in ch-4 sp, ch 3, 2 dc in next ch-4 sp, dc in next dc; rep from * to last square, ch 1, sk 1, dc in top of ch sp at end of row, turn.

ROW 4: Ch 3, ch 1, sk ch, dc in dc, ch 1, sk dc, dc in dc, 3 dc in ch-3 sp, *dc in dc, ch 1, sk 1 dc, dc in dc, ch 1, sk ch, dc in dc, ch 1, sk dc, dc in dc, 3 dc in ch-3 sp; repeat from * to last 2 squares, ch 1, sk 1 dc, dc in dc, ch 1, sk ch, dc in top of ch sp at end of row, turn.

ROW 5: Ch 4, sk 1 ch or dc, dc in dc, *ch 1, sk 1 ch or dc, dc in dc; rep from * across, turn.

ROWS 6–7: Ch 4, sk ch, dc in dc, *ch 1, sk ch, dc in dc; rep from * across, turn.

135 Irish Sprout

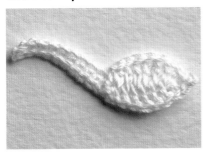

Foundation: Ch 20, sl st in 11th ch from hk, turn.

ROW 1: (Sc, hdc, 5 dc) in circle, ch 2, sl st in 2nd ch from hk, (5 dc, hdc, sc) between sts already in circle to create leaf shape, sc in remaining ch of Foundation ch.

136 Irish Berry

Foundation: Ch 1.

ROW 1: Ch 3, 5 dc in Foundation ch from hk, remove hk and reinsert into top of 1st and last dc, yo, pull through all lps, insert hk in Foundation ch, yo, pull through both lps.

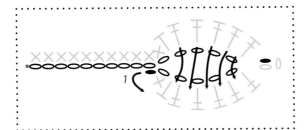

137 Irish Leaf

Work every st in the front half of each ch or st, except the last 5 sts of Row 1, which are worked in the back half of the st, and the sc sts in Row 5, which are worked as you normally would work the first row of sc in a foundation ch.

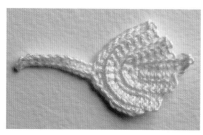

Foundation: Ch 7, turn.

ROW 1: Ch 1, sc in the 2nd ch from hk and ea ch to the last ch, 5 sc in last ch, working in the other half of the chs, 4 sc, turn.

ROW 2: Ch 1, 5 sc, 2 sc in ea of the next 3 sts, 5 sc, turn.

ROW 3: Ch 1, 6 sc, (2 sc in next st, sc) 3 times, 3 sc, turn.

ROW 4: Ch 1, 7 sc, 2 sc in next st, sc, (2 sc in next st) twice, 6 sc, turn.

ROW 5: Ch 1, 8 sc, hdc, dc, ch 11, sc in 2nd ch from hk and next 9 ch, continuing along the outer edge of the leaf, dc, hdc, 7 sc, weave in ends.

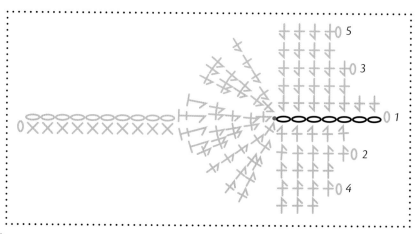

138 Irish Rose

Note: The arrows in the chart indicate the sc to work into for Rows 4 and 6.

Foundation: Ch 4, turn.

RND 1: 14 dc in 4th ch from hk, sl st in top of ch-4, do not turn.

RND 2: Sc in dc, (ch 5, sk 2, sc in next dc) 5 times, working last sc in top of Foundation ch-4, do not turn.

RND 3: *(Sc, hdc, 5 dc, hdc, sc) in ch-5 sp; rep from * in ea ch-5 sp, do not turn.

RND 4: Sc in 2 strands of the back post of 1st sc of Rnd 2, (ch 7, sc in 2 strands of the back post of next sc of Rnd 2) 5 times, working the last sc in the 1st sc of the row, do not turn.

RND 5: *(Sc, hdc, 7 dc, hdc, sc) in ch-7 sp; rep from * in each ch-7 sp, do not turn.

RND 6: Sc in 2 strands of the back post of 1st sc of Rnd 4, (ch 9, sc in 2 strands of the back post of next sc of Rnd 4) 5 times, working the last sc in the 1st sc of the row, do not turn.

RND 7: *(Sc, hdc, 9 dc, hdc, sc) in ch-9 sp; rep from * in each ch-9 sp, do not turn.

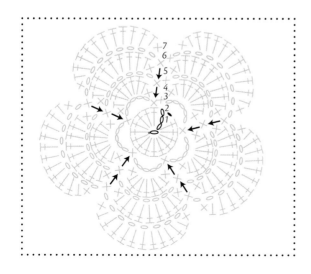

Snowflakes

Note: Snowflake patterns require you to slip stitch in the same place more than once. For clarity, I have added a letter in parentheses (X) after a slip stitch that will be worked repeatedly.

139 Small Snowflake

Foundation: Ch 1, do not turn.
RND 1: Ch 3, dc in 4th ch from hk, ch 2, (2 dc, ch 2) 5 times in 4th ch from hk, sl st in top of ch-3 at beg of rnd, do not turn.
RND 2: *Ch 4, sc in next ch-2 sp, ch 6, sl st in 4th ch from hk (A), ch 9, sl st in 3rd ch from hk, ch 5, sl st in (A), ch 3, sl st in (A) again, ch 2, sc in same ch-2 sp as previous sc; rep from * 5 times, do not turn.

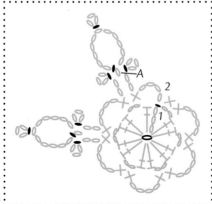

140 Large Snowflake

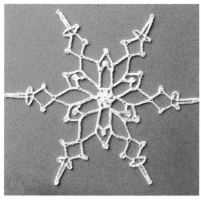

Foundation: Ch 1, do not turn.

RND 1: Ch 3, dc in 4th ch from hk, ch 2, (2 dc, ch 2) 5 times in 4th ch from hk, sl st in top of ch-3 at beg of rnd, do not turn.

RND 2: *Ch 11, sl st in 5th ch from hk, ch 6, sc in next ch-2 sp; rep from * around, do not turn.

RND 3: Sl st in 2nd, 3rd, 4th and 5th ch of 1st ch-11 sp of Rnd 2, ch 9, sl st in 4th ch from hk, ch 3, *dc in 3rd ch of ch-6 sp, ch 13, sl st in 4th ch from hk, ch 10, sl st in 7th ch from hk (A), ch 8, sl st in 3rd ch from hk, ch 5, sl st in (A), ch 6, sl st in (A), ch 7, sl st in 4th ch from hk, ch 3, sl st in 6th ch of ch-11, ch 5, dc in ch-6 of Rnd 2, ch 6, sl st in 3rd ch from hk, ch 3; rep from * around, sl st in 5th sl st at beg of round.

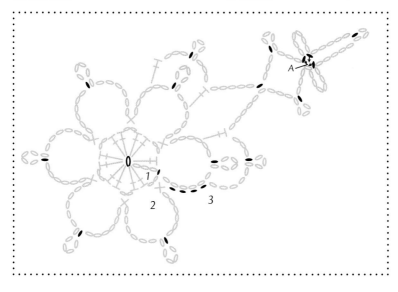

141 Diamond Snowflake

Foundation: Ch 1, do not turn.

RND 1: Ch 3, dc in 4th ch from hk, ch 2, (2 dc, ch 2) 5 times in 4th ch from hk, sl st in top of ch-3 at beg of rnd, do not turn.

RND 2: Ch 4, (sc, ch 3, sc) in next ch-2 sp, *ch 3, (sc, ch 3, sc) in next ch-2 sp; rep from * around, do not turn.

RND 3: Ch 5, sk ch-4 sp, 6 tr in next ch-3 sp, *sk next ch-3 sp, 6 tr in next ch-3 sp; rep from * around, ending the last rep with 5 tr in next ch-3 sp instead of 6 tr, sl st in 3rd ch of ch-5 at beg of rnd, do not turn.

RND 4: Ch 5, *make a 6-tr cluster in the next shell, ch 6, sl st in 6th ch from hk (A), ch 9, sl st in 4th ch from hk, ch 5, sl st in (A), ch 5, sl st in (A), ch 9; rep from * around, sl st in (A) of next leg of snowflake.

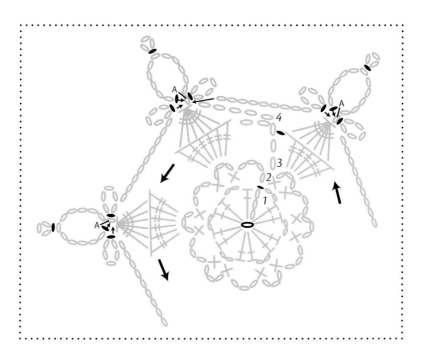

142 Crystal Feathered Snowflake

Foundation: Ch 1, do not turn.

RND 1: Ch 3, dc in 4th ch from hk, ch 2, (2 dc, ch 2) 5 times in 4th ch from hk, sl st in top of ch-3 at beg of rnd, do not turn.

RND 2: Ch 1, sc in top of ch-3 and 1st dc in rnd 1, (sc, ch 1, sc), in ch-2 sp, *sc in next 2 sts, (sc, ch 1, sc) in ch-2 sp; rep from * around, sl st in ch-1, do not turn.

RND 3: Ch 3, sk 1, dc in next 2 sts, *ch 3, sk ch-sp, dc in next 4 sts; rep from * 5 times, ch 3, sk ch-sp, dc in next st, sl st in top of ch-3, do not turn.

RND 4: Sl st in 1st and 2nd dc, *(sc, ch 6, sc) in ch-3 sp, ch 7, sl st in 4th ch from hk, ch 3; rep from * 6 times, sl st in sc at beg of row, do not turn.

RND 5: Sl st in 1st 3 ch of ch-6, ch 3, (dc, ch 2, 2dc) in same ch-6 sp, *ch 6, (2 dc, ch 2, 2 dc) in next ch-6 sp; rep from * 5 times, ch 6, sl st in top of ch-3, do not turn.

RND 6: Ch 3, *sk 1, dc in dc, 4 dc in ch-2 sp, dc in dc, sk 1, 8 dc in ch-6 sp; rep from * around, sl st in top of ch-3, do not turn.

RND 7: Sl st in next 2 sts, *ch 9, sl st in 3rd ch from hk, ch 5, sl st in 1st ch of ch-9 (A), ch 10, sl st in 3rd ch from hk, ch 5, sl st in 2nd ch of ch-10 (B), ch 8, sl st in 3rd ch from hk, ch 3, sl st in 2nd ch of ch-8 (C), ch 6, sl st in 3rd ch from hk, ch 3, sl st in (C) ch 6, sl st in 3rd ch from hk, ch 3, sl st in (C), ch 1, sl st in (B), ch 8, sl st in 3rd ch from hk, ch 5, sl st in (B), ch 1, sl st in (A), ch 8, sl st in 3rd ch from hk, ch 5, sl st in (A), ch 11, sl st in 4th ch from hk, ch 7, sl st in center of next 4-dc shell of Rnd 6; rep from * around.

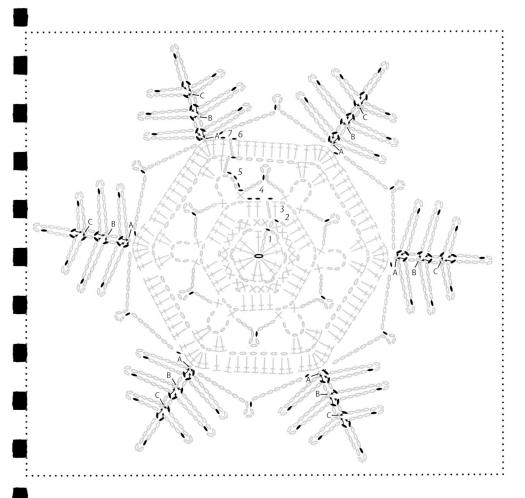

Tunisian Crochet

Tunisian, or afghan, stitch is worked on a long crochet hook with a stopper at one end, similar to a knitting needle. The stitches are worked onto the hook from right to left, then worked off of the hook from left to right, without ever turning the work to form stitches on the back side of the piece. In the following stitch patterns, each row is in two parts: Part A of a row is worked from right to left as you add stitches to the hook, and Part B of a row is worked from left to right as you work stitches off of the hook. The following key and stitch guide describes the symbols and stitches used for Tunisian Crochet.

Chain (ch) - yarn over, pull through loop.

Tunisian single crochet in the back of the stitch or chain (Tsc tbl) - insert hook into the back of the stitch or chain, yarn over, pull through stitch or chain.

Tunisian Simple Stitch (Tss) - insert hook into the vertical bar, yarn over, pull through vertical bar.

Row B yarn over - wrap the yarn around the hook, pull through the next 2 loops on the hook.

Yarn over between stitches - wrap the yarn around the hook.

Tunisian single crochet through the fabric (Tsc tf) - insert the hook through the fabric, behind the vertical bar through to the back side of the work, yarn over, pull through the fabric.

Tunisian Purl Stitch in the back loop (Tps tbl) - bring the yarn to the front of the work, insert the hook into the back loop of the stitch or chain, wrap the yarn under and over the hook to make a yarn over, pull through the loop.

Tunisian Purl Stitch (Tps) - bring the yarn to the front of the work, insert the hook into the vertical bar, wrap the yarn under and over the hook to make a yarn over, pull through the loop.

Tunisian Simple Stitch in the horizontal bar (Tss thzb) - insert the hook into the horizontal strand of yarn at the top of the piece before the next vertical bar (through the top strand only, unless indicated otherwise), yarn over, pull through horizontal strand(s).

Tunisian Half Double Crochet (Thdc) - yarn over, insert the hook into the vertical bar, yarn over, pull through the bar, yarn over, pull through 2 loops.

Tunisian Half Double Crochet in the back loop (Thdc tbl) - yarn over, insert the hook into the back half of the stitch or chain, yarn over, pull through stitch or chain, yarn over, pull through 2 loops.

Tunisian Half Double Crochet in the horizontal bar (Thdc thzb) - yarn over, insert the hook into the horizontal strand of yarn at the top of the piece before the next vertical bar (through the top strand only unless indicated otherwise), yarn over, pull through bar, yarn over, pull through two loops.

Tunisian Double Crochet (Tdc) - yarn over, insert the hook into the vertical bar, yarn over, pull through the bar, yarn over, pull through 2 loops, yarn over, pull through 1 loop.

Tunisian Double Crochet in the back loop (Tdc tbl) - yarn over, insert the hook into the back half of the stitch or chain, yarn over, pull through stitch or chain, yarn over, pull through 2 loops, yarn over, pull through 1 loop.

Tunisian Half Double Crochet 4-Stitch Bobble (Thdc 4stB) - (yarn over, insert hook into the vertical bar, yarn over, pull through bar, yarn over, pull through 2 loops) repeat 4 times in the same vertical bar, yarn over, pull through 4 loops.

143 Basic Tunisian Stitch

Any number of stitches

Foundation: Ch any number of sts.

ROW 1A: Ch 1, Tsc tbl in 2nd ch from hk and ea ch across.

ROW 1B: Ch 1, *yo, pull through next 2 lps on hk; rep from * across.

ROW 2A: Ch 1, Tss in ea st across.

ROW 2B: Ch 1, *yo, pull through next 2 lps on hk; rep from * across.

Rep Rows 2a and 2b to cont patt.

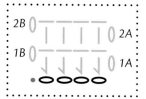

144 Tunisian Knit Stitch

Any number of stitches

Foundation: Ch any number of sts.

ROW 1A: Ch 1, Tsc tbl in 2nd ch from hk and ea ch across.

ROW 1B: Ch 1, *yo, pull through next 2 lps on hk; rep from * across.

ROW 2A: Ch 1, Tsc tf in ea st across.

ROW 2B: Ch 1, *yo, pull through next 2 lps on hk; rep from * across.

Rep Rows 2a and 2b to cont patt.

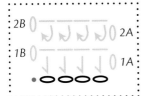

145 Tunisian Purl Stitch

Any number of stitches

Foundation: Ch any number of sts.

ROW 1A: Ch 1, Tps tbl in 2nd ch from hk and ea ch across.

ROW 1B: Ch 1, *yo, pull through next 2 lps on hk; rep from * across.

ROW 2A: Ch 1, Tps in ea st across.

ROW 2B: Ch 1, *yo, pull through next 2 lps on hk; rep from * across.

Rep Rows 2a and 2b to cont patt.

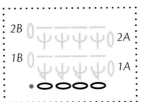

146 Alternating Twisted Tunisian

Any number of stitches

Foundation: Ch any number of sts.

ROW 1A: Ch 1, Tsc tbl in 2nd ch from hk and ea ch across.

ROW 1B: Ch 1, *yo, pull through next 2 lps on hk; rep from * across.

ROW 2A: Ch 1, Tss thzb in ea st across.

ROW 2B: Ch 1, *yo, pull through next 2 lps on hk; rep from * across.

ROW 3A: Ch 1, Tss in ea st across.

ROW 3B: Ch 1, *yo, pull through next 2 lps on hk; rep from * across.

Rep Rows 2a through 3b to cont patt.

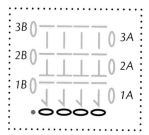

147 Chain One Basic

Any number of stitches

Foundation: Ch any number of sts.

ROW 1A: Ch 1, Tsc tbl in 2nd ch from hk, ch 1, *Tsc tbl in the next ch, ch 1; rep from * across.

ROW 1B: Ch 1, *yo, pull through next 2 lps on hk; rep from * across.

ROW 2A: Ch 1, *Tss thzb, ch 1; rep from * across.

ROW 2B: Ch 1, *yo, pull through next 2 lps on hk; rep from * across.

Rep Rows 2a and 2b to cont patt.

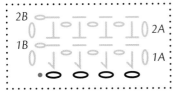

148 Half Double Crochet

Any number of stitches

Foundation: Ch any number of sts.

ROW 1A: Ch 2, Thdc tbl in 2nd ch from hk and ea ch across.

ROW 1B: Ch 1, *yo, pull through next 2 lps on hk; rep from * across.

ROW 2A: Ch 2, Thdc thzb in ea st across.

ROW 2B: Ch 1, *yo, pull through next 2 lps on hk; rep from * across.

Rep Rows 2a and 2b to cont patt.

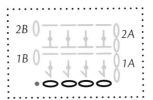

149 Tunisian Double Crochet

Any number of stitches

Foundation: Ch any number of sts.

ROW 1A: Ch 3, Tdc tbl in 4th ch from hk and ea ch across.

ROW 1B: Ch 1, *yo, pull through next 2 lps on hk; rep from * across.

ROW 2A: Ch 3, Tdc in ea st across.

ROW 2B: Ch 1, *yo, pull through next 2 lps on hk; rep from * across.

Rep Rows 2a and 2b to cont patt.

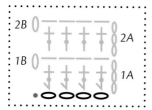

150 Relaxed Tunisian

Any number of stitches, plus 1

Foundation: Ch any number of sts, plus 1.

ROW 1A: Ch 1, Tsc tbl in 2nd ch from hk and ea ch across.

ROW 1B: *Ch 1, yo, pull through next 2 lps on hk; rep from * across.

ROW 2A: Tss thzb across.

ROW 2B: *Ch 1, yo, pull through next 2 lps on hk; rep from * across.

Rep Rows 2a and 2b to cont patt.

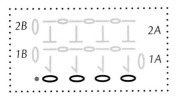

151 Tunisian Crossed Grid

Multiple of 3 stitches

Foundation: Ch a multiple of 3 sts.

ROW 1A: Ch 3, Tsc tbl in 6th ch from hk, *ch 2, sk 2, Tsc tbl; rep from * across.

ROW 1B: Ch 3, yo, pull through next 2 lps on hk, *ch 2, yo, pull through next 2 lps on hk; rep from * across.

ROW 2A: *Ch 2, Tss; rep from * across.

ROW 2B: Ch 3, yo, pull through next 2 lps on hk, *ch 2, yo, pull through next 2 lps on hk; rep from * across.

Rep Rows 2a and 2b to cont patt.

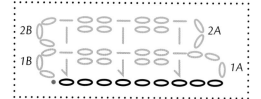

152 Honeycomb

Multiple of 3 stitches

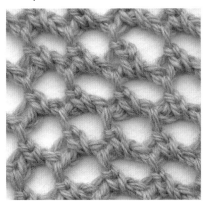

Foundation: Ch a multiple of 3 sts, turn.

ROW 1A: Ch 3, Tsc tbl in 6th ch from hk, *ch 2, sk 2, Tsc tbl; rep from * across.

ROW 1B: Ch 4, yo, pull through next 2 lps on hk, *ch 2, yo, pull through next 2 lps on hk; rep from * across.

ROW 2A: Ch 3, Tss in ch sp at start of row, *ch 2, Tss in next ch sp; rep from * across, ending with Tss in ch sp at end of row.

ROW 2B: Ch 4, yo, pull through next 2 lps on hk, *ch 2, yo, pull through next 2 lps on hk; rep from * across.

Rep Rows 2a and 2b to cont patt.

On the last B row: Ch 1, *yo, pull through next 2 lps on hk; rep from * across.

153 Shells

A multiple of 3 stitches, plus 1

Foundation: Ch a multiple of 3 sts, plus 1.
ROW 1A: Ch 2, Thdc tbl in 3rd ch from hk 3 times, *sk 2, Thdc tbl in next ch 4 times; rep from * across.

ROW 1B: Ch 1, *yo, pull through next 2 lps on hk; rep from * across.

ROW 2A: Ch 3, Thdc 4 times in ea sp between shells.

ROW 2B: Ch 1, *yo, pull through next 2 lps on hk; rep from * across.

ROW 3A: Ch 3, Thdc 3 times in base of ch-3, Thdc 4 times in ea sp between shells, Thdc 4 times in last st of row.

ROW 3B: Ch 1, *yo, pull through next 2 lps on hk; rep from * across.

Rep Rows 2a through 3b to cont patt.

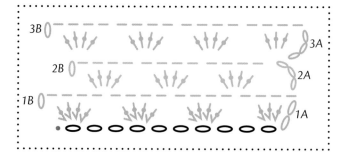

154 Cluster Rows

A multiple of 5 stitches

Foundation: Ch a multiple of 5 sts.

ROW 1A: Ch 3, Tdc tbl in 4th ch from hk and ea ch across.

ROW 1B: Ch 2, yo, pull through next 6 lps on hk, *ch 3, yo, pull through next 6 lps on hk; rep from * to last 2 lps, ch 3, pull through 2 lps.

ROW 2A: *(Tss, ch 1) 4 times in next ch sp, (Tss, ch 1) in top of cluster; rep from * across, ending with Tss, ch 1, in ch sp at end of row.

ROW 2B: Ch 1, *yo, pull through next 2 lps on hk; rep from * across.

ROW 3A: Ch 3, Tdc tbl in ea st across.

ROW 3B: Ch 2, yo, pull through next 6 lps on hk, *ch 3, yo, pull through next 6 lps on hk; rep from * to last 2 lps, ch 3, pull through 2 lps.

Rep Rows 2a through 3b to cont patt.

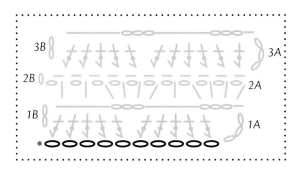

155 Bobbles

A multiple of 6 stitches, plus 2

Foundation: Ch a multiple of 6 sts, plus 2.

ROW 1A: Ch 2, Thdc tbl in 3rd ch from hk and ea ch across.

ROW 1B: Ch 1, *yo, pull through next 2 lps on hk; rep from * across.

ROW 2A: Ch 2, 2 Thdc, *Thdc 4stB, 5 Thdc; rep from * across.

ROW 2B: Ch 1, *yo, pull through next 2 lps on hk; rep from * across.

ROW 3A: Ch 2, *5 Thdc, Thdc 4stB; rep from * to last 2 sts, 2 Thdc.

ROW 3B: Ch 1, *yo, pull through next 2 lps on hk; rep from * across.

Rep Rows 2a through 3b to cont patt.

156 Crossed Stitches

A multiple of 2 stitches.

Foundation: Ch a multiple of 2 sts, turn.

ROW 1A: Ch 1, Tsc tbl in 2nd ch from hk and ea ch across.

ROW 1B: Ch 1, *yo, pull through next 2 lps on hk; rep from * across.

ROW 2A: Ch 1, *sk 1, Tss, Tss into st just skipped; rep from * across.

ROW 2B: Ch 1, *yo, pull through next 2 lps on hk; rep from * across.

Rep Rows 2a and 2b to cont patt.

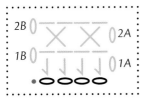

CroKnit

CroKnit, also known as double-ending crocheting, Cro-knit or Crochenit, is worked in a similar method to Tunisian crochet, and even uses the same symbols, except the work is turned and worked from both ends of a double-ended hook using two balls of yarn. In the following patterns the two balls of yarn are referred to as Yarn 1 and Yarn 2. These stitches can be worked in one or more colors. The following samples are worked in two colors, which is recommended when learning this technique.

157 Basic Back and Forth

Any number of stitches

Foundation: With Yarn 1, ch any number of sts, turn.

ROW 1A: With Yarn 1, ch 1, Tsc tbl in 2nd ch from hk and ea ch across, turn.

ROW 1B: With Yarn 2, ch 1, *yo, pull through next 2 lps on hk; rep from * across, turn.

ROW 2A: With Yarn 1, ch 1, Tss in ea st across, turn.

ROW 2B: With Yarn 2, ch 1, *yo, pull through next 2 lps on hk; rep from * across, turn.

Rep Rows 2a and 2b to cont patt.

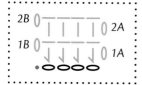

158 Ribbing

Any number of stitches

Foundation: With Yarn 1, ch any number of sts, turn.

ROW 1A: With Yarn 1, ch 1, Tsc tbl in 2nd ch from hk and ea ch across, turn.

ROW 1B: With Yarn 2, ch 1, *yo, pull through next 2 lps on hk; rep from * across, turn.

ROW 2A: With Yarn 1, ch 1, Tsc tf in ea st across, turn.

ROW 2B: With Yarn 2, ch 1, *yo, pull through next 2 lps on hk; rep from * across, turn.

Rep Rows 2a and 2b to cont patt.

159 Double Crochet/ Single Crochet

Any number of stitches

Foundation: With Yarn 1, ch any number of sts, turn.

ROW 1A: With Yarn 1, ch 1, Tsc tbl in 2nd ch from hk and ea ch across, turn.

ROW 1B: With Yarn 2, ch 1, *yo, pull through next 2 lps on hk; rep from * across, turn.

ROW 2A: With Yarn 1, ch 3, Tdc in ea st across, turn.

ROW 2B: With Yarn 2, ch 1, *yo, pull through next 2 lps on hk; rep from * across, turn.

ROW 3A: With Yarn 1, ch 1, Tss in ea st across, turn.

ROW 3B: With Yarn 2, ch 1, *yo, pull through next 2 lps on hk; rep from * across, turn.

Rep Rows 2a through 3b to cont patt.

160 Pillars and Windows

A multiple of 3 stitches, plus 1

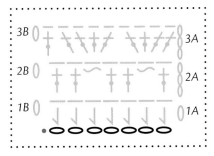

Foundation: With Yarn 1, ch a multiple of 3 sts, plus 1, turn.

ROW 1A: With Yarn 1, ch 1, Tsc tbl in 2nd ch from hk and ea ch across, turn.

ROW 1B: With Yarn 2, ch 1, *yo, pull through next 2 lps on hk; rep from * across, do not turn.

ROW 2A: With Yarn 2, ch 3, Tdc, *yo, 2 Tdc; rep from * across, turn.

ROW 2B: With Yarn 1, ch 1, *yo, pull through next 2 lps on hk; rep from * across, do not turn.

ROW 3A: With Yarn 1, ch 3, Tdc 4 times in ea space between pairs of Tdc from Row 2A, ending with Tdc in ch sp at end of row, turn.

ROW 3B: With Yarn 2, ch 1, *yo, pull through next 2 lps on hk; rep from * across, do not turn.

Rep Rows 2a through 3b to cont patt.

161 Eyelet

A multiple of 3 stitches, plus 2

Foundation: With Yarn 1, ch a multiple of 3 sts, plus 2, turn.

ROW 1A: With Yarn 1, ch 2, yo twice, Tsc tbl in 4th ch from hk, *yo twice, sk 2, Tsc tbl; rep from * across, turn.

ROW 1B: With Yarn 2, ch 1, *yo, pull through next 2 lps on hk; rep from * across, turn.

ROW 2A: With Yarn 1, ch 2, *yo twice, Tss in space between sts; rep from * across, turn.

ROW 2B: With Yarn 2, ch 1, *yo, pull through next 2 lps on hk; rep from * across, turn.

Rep Rows 2a and 2b to cont patt.

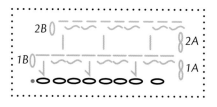

162 Shell Waves

A multiple of 7 stitches, plus 1

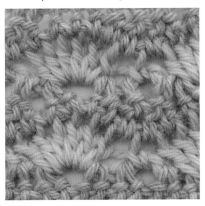

Foundation: With Yarn 1, ch a multiple of 7 sts, plus 1, turn.

ROW 1A: With Yarn 1, ch 3, Tdc tbl in 4th ch from hk and ea ch across, turn.

ROW 1B: With Yarn 2, ch 2, yo, pull through next 2 lps on hk, *ch 1, yo, pull through next 2 lps on hk; rep from * across, turn.

ROW 2A: With Yarn 1, ch 1, *Tss in ch sp, sk 1 ch sp, Tdc in next ch sp 6 times; rep from * across, end with Tss in ch sp at end of row, turn.

ROW 2B: With Yarn 2, ch 2, yo, pull through next 2 lps on hk, *ch 1, yo, pull through next 2 lps on hk; rep from * across, turn.

ROW 3A: With Yarn 1, ch 3, *Tdc in ch sp, Thdc in next ch sp, Tss in next 3 ch sp, Thdc in next ch sp, Tdc in next ch sp; rep from * across, turn.

ROW 3B: With Yarn 2, ch 2, yo, pull through next 2 lps on hk, *ch 1, yo, pull through next 2 lps on hk; rep from * across, turn.

Rep Rows 2a through 3b to cont patt.

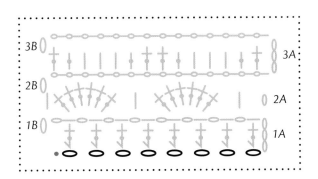

CHAPTER THREE

Basic Projects

A scarf, a hat, a sweater ... here is a collection of basic projects to make with crochet. These are timeless patterns that you can make as shown, or you can substitute pattern stitches from Chapter Two to make a personalized design. This is just a small sampling of the many things you can make with crochet.

Basic Bag

Bags are great projects to make because you can experiment with colors and patterns without worrying about fit. Plus, when the bag is finished you have a wonderful, useful project to carry more yarn! This basic bag can be as simple or as complex as you want to make it. Use an easy stitch pattern and some variegated yarn, as I did, for an elegant look.

The project shown at left was made using Cascade Yarn Cascade 220 (100% wool, 3½oz./100g, 220yd./200m) colors 9325 (A) and 9923 (B).

SKILL LEVEL

Intermediate

FINISHED SIZE

Approx. 15"× 10" (38cm × 25cm), excluding strap

YARN

1 (3½oz./100g, 220yd./200m) skein solid worsted weight yarn (A)

1 (3½oz./100g, 220yd./200m) skein variegated worsted weight yarn (B)

HOOK

U.S. H (5mm) crochet hook

NOTIONS

Sewing needle and thread to match yarn A

Stitch marker

Straight pins

Tapestry needle

14" (36cm) zipper

16" × 22" (41cm × 56cm) piece of fabric for lining and matching thread (optional)

GAUGE

16 sc and 18 rows = 4" (10cm)

207

See Crochet Abbreviations on page 245.

Bottom

With yarn A, ch 11.

ROW 1: Ch 1, sc in 2nd ch from hk and ea ch across, turn—10 sts.

ROWS 2-49: Ch 1, sc in ea st across, turn—10 sts.

Sides

RND 1: Ch 1, sc in ea st across (10 sc), working across long edge of Bottom, sc in the end of ea row (49 sc), sc in ea ch of foundation ch (10 sc), sc in the end of ea row along the remaining side (49 sc), do not join—118 sts. Work in a spiral, placing a marker in first st of rnd, moving marker up as work progresses.

RNDS 2-6: Sc in ea st around—118 sts. Fasten off yarn A, join yarn B.

Body

RND 1: *Sc in ea of next 2 sts, dc in ea of next 2 sts; rep from * around, ending with sc in ea of last 2 sts, do not join, continue to work in a spiral—118 sts.

RND 2: *Dc in ea of next 2 sts, sc in ea of next 2 sts; rep from * around, ending with dc in ea of last 2 sts—118 sts.

Rep Rnds 1-2 until you don't have enough yarn left for a complete row. At end of last rnd, fasten off yarn B, join yarn A.

With yarn A, work 2 rnds sc. At end of last rnd, sl st in next sc to join. Secure last st. Weave in ends.

Strap (make 3)

With yarn A, ch 150.

ROW 1: Ch 1, sc in 2nd ch from hook and ea ch across—149 sc.

Cut the yarn and pull through the last loop, but don't weave in the ends.

Assembly

Pin the zipper in place along the top opening of the bag and sew in place with the sewing needle and matching sewing thread.

Braided Shoulder Strap

Beg with the ends of the Straps that don't have yarn tails, loop one end of one Strap so you have a 1"–1½" (3cm–4cm) long loop. Using a scrap of yarn and the tapestry needle, sew the loop in place. Place the ends of the other two Straps under the loop and sew the Straps together.

Braid the Straps, keeping the Straps flat so they don't twist as you braid them. Pin the ends of the Straps to the side edges of the bag and adjust to the desired length, marking any shortened length with a pin through the braid. If the braid is long enough as is, sew it in place at both sides of the bag. If the braid is too long, cut the braid about 1" (3cm) from the pin marking, and unravel the ends of the Straps and use the ends to sew the Braided Shoulder Strap to the side of the bag. Sew the other end to the other side of the bag.

Lining (optional)

Fold the 16" × 22" (41cm × 56cm) piece of fabric with RS together so it is 11" × 16" (28cm × 41cm). Sew ½" (1cm) seams along the 11" (28cm) sides. Place the lining in the bag to make sure it fits. It is better to have a little extra lining because a small liner will pull on the bag. Fold under the top raw edge of the lining. Remove the lining and press the folded raw edge. Pin the lining in the bag and sew it to the zipper along the stitches used to sew the zipper to the bag.

Basic Double Crochet Scarf

This scarf is a great first project, and it's also a great project to turn to for a quick and easy gift. Try using novelty yarn or yarn that gradually changes color throughout the skein for a completely different look.

The project shown at left was made using
Berroco Suede (100% nylon, 1¾oz./50g,
120yd./110m) color 3745, Calamity Jane.

SKILL LEVEL
Intermediate

FINISHED SIZE
Approx. 5" × 62" (13cm × 157cm) without fringe

YARN
3 (1¾oz./50g, 120yd./110m) skeins worsted weight yarn

HOOK
U.S. H (5mm) crochet hook

NOTIONS
Tapestry needle

GAUGE
16 dc and 8 rows = 4"(10cm)

See Crochet Abbreviations on page 245.

Cut 80 12" (30cm) strands of yarn and set them aside for the fringe.

Scarf
Ch 20.
ROW 1: Ch 3 (counts as first dc), dc in 4th ch from hk and ea ch across, turn—21 sts.
ROW 2: Ch 3 (counts as first dc), dc in ea st across, turn—21 sts.
Rep Row 2 until scarf is as long as you wish or all the yarn is used. Secure last st.
Weave in ends.

Fringe
Beg at one end of the scarf, take 2 strands of fringe and fold them in half. Insert the
hook into the first st at the corner of the scarf, drape the folded yarn over the crochet
hook and draw it through the fabric about 1" (3cm). Wrap the fringe ends over the
hook like a yarn over, then pull the ends through the folded yarn. Tighten the knot
created. Repeat the process 20 times on ea short edge of the scarf.

Tip

*By cutting the fringe pieces before you begin
the scarf, you can crochet the remaining
yarn and not worry if you'll have enough
left over for the fringe.*

Basic Single Crochet Hat

This quick and easy-to-make hat is a great project in any yarn and any color, and it stretches enough to fit most head sizes. This project easily lends itself to colorwork patterns because it is worked in the round in single crochet, which is ideal for color changes.

The project shown at left was made using Brown Sheep Lamb's Pride Worsted (85% wool/15% mohair, 4oz./113g, 190yd./174m), color M07, Sable.

SKILL LEVEL

Easy

FINISHED SIZE

Approx. 22" (56cm) circumference

YARN

1 (4oz./113g, 190yd./174m) skein worsted weight yarn

HOOK

U.S. H (5mm) crochet hook

NOTIONS

Stitch marker

Tapestry needle

GAUGE

16 sc and 18 rows = 4" (10cm)

See Crochet Abbreviations on page 245.

Ch 2.

RND 1: 7 sc in 2nd ch from hk, do not join—7 sc. Work in a spiral, placing a marker in first st of rnd, moving marker up as work progresses.

RND 2: 2 sc in each sc around—14 sc.

RND 3: *Sc in next st, 2 sc in next st; rep from * 6 more times—21 sc.

RND 4: *Sc in each of next 2 sts, 2 sc in next st; rep from * around—28 sts.

RND 5: *Sc in each of next 3 sts, 2 sc in next st; rep from * around—35 sts.

RND 6: *Sc in each of next 4 sts, 2 sc in next st; rep from * around—42 sts.

RND 7: *Sc in each of next 5 sts, 2 sc in next st; rep from * around—49 sts.

RND 8: *Sc in each of next 6 sts, 2 sc in next st; rep from * around—56 sts.

RND 9: *Sc in each of next 7 sts, 2 sc in next st; rep from * around—63 sts.

RND 10: *Sc in each of next 8 sts, 2 sc in next st; rep from * around—70 sts.

RND 11: *Sc in each of next 9 sts, 2 sc in next st; rep from * around—77 sts.

RND 12: *Sc in each of next 10 sts, 2 sc in next st; rep from * around—84 sts.

RNDS 13-42: Sc in each st around.

Secure last st. Weave in ends.

Turn up brim about 1½" (4cm).

Tip

This hat is easy to work for different sized heads. Just keep increasing until the measurement around the last round is approximately 1½" (4cm) less than the recipient's head circumference. Then work even without increases until the hat measures approximately 9"–10" (23cm–25cm) from the cast-on edge.

Basic Sleeveless Blouse

This light and airy summer blouse is great over a tank top or bathing suit. Work it in a less lacy stitch pattern if you want to wear it alone, or make it longer for a different look.

The project shown at left was made using Rowan Yarn 4 Ply Cotton (100% cotton, 1¾oz./50g, 186yd./170m), color 120, Orchid.

SKILL LEVEL
Intermediate

FINISHED SIZE
Finished Bust: 36 (40, 43, 46)" [91 (102, 109, 117)cm]

Length: 20 (20, 22, 22)" [51 (51, 56, 56)cm]

To fit bust sizes: 34 (37, 40, 43)" (86 [94, 102, 109]cm)

YARN
4 (4, 5, 6) (1¾oz./50g, 186yd./170m) skeins sport weight yarn

HOOK
U.S. F (3.75mm) crochet hook

NOTIONS
Tapestry needle

6 ½" (1cm) buttons

GAUGE
24 sts and 11 rows in pattern = 4" (10cm)

Special Stitch

V-st: (Dc, ch, dc) in same st or space.

See Crochet Abbreviations on page 245.

Back

Ch 104 (113, 122, 131).

ROW 1 (RS): Ch 4 (counts as dc, ch 1), dc in 5th ch from hk, *sk next 2 ch, V-st in next ch; rep from * across, turn—35 (38, 41, 44) V-sts.

ROW 2: Ch 4 (counts as dc, ch 1), sk next ch-1 space, *dc in ea of next 2 dc, ch 1, sk next ch-1 space; rep from * across, ending with dc in 3rd ch of turning ch, turn—35 (38, 41, 44) ch-1 spaces.

ROW 3: Ch 4 (counts as dc, ch 1), dc in next ch-1 space, V-st in ea ch-1 space across, turn—35 (38, 41, 44) V-sts.

Rep Rows 2–3 11 (11, 12, 12) times—27 (27, 29, 29) rows.

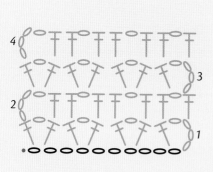

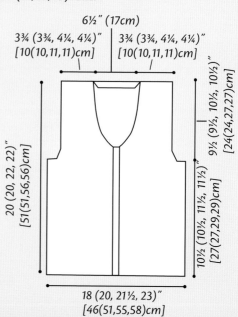

6½" (17cm)

3¾ (3¾, 4¼, 4¼)"
[10(10,11,11)cm]

3¾ (3¾, 4¼, 4¼)"
[10(10,11,11)cm]

9½ (9½, 10½, 10½)"
[24(24,27,27)cm]

20 (20, 22, 22)"
[51(51,56,56)cm]

10½ (10½, 11½, 11½)"
[27(27,29,29)cm]

18 (20, 21½, 23)"
[46(51,55,58)cm]

Shape Armholes

ROW 1 (1ST DEC ROW): Sk first dc, sl st in ea of next 6 sts (2 reps and first st of 3rd rep of Row 3 patt), ch 3, sk next ch-1 space, dc in ea of next 2 dc, *ch 1, sk next ch-1 space, dc in ea of next 2 dc; rep from * across to within last 3 ch-1 spaces, sk next ch-1 space, dc in next dc, turn—29 (32, 35, 38) ch-1 spaces.

ROW 2 (2ND DEC ROW): Ch 3, sk first 3 dc, dc in next ch-1 space, work V-st in ea ch-1 space across to within last ch-1 space, dc in next ch-1 space, sk next 2 dc, dc in top of ch-3 turning ch, turn—27 (30, 33, 36) V-sts.

ROW 3 (3RD DEC ROW): Ch 3, sk first 2 dc, dc in next dc, *ch 1, sk next ch-1 space, dc in ea of next 2 dc; rep from * across to within last ch-1 space, ch 1, sk next ch-1 space, dc in next dc, sk next dc, dc in top of turning ch, turn—27 (30, 33, 36) ch-1 spaces.

Upper Back

ROW 1: Ch 3 (counts as dc), V-st in ea ch-1 space across, dc in top of ch-3 turning ch, turn—27 (30, 33, 36) V-sts plus dc at ea end of row.

ROW 2: Ch 3 (counts as dc), sk first dc, dc in next dc, *ch 1, sk next ch-1 space, dc in ea of next 2 dc; rep from * across, ending with last dc in top of ch-3 turning ch, turn—27 (30, 33, 36) ch-1 spaces.

Rep Rows 1-2 8 (8, 9, 9) times, then rep Row 1 once—19 (19, 21, 21) rows.

Left Shoulder

ROW 1: Ch 3 (counts as dc), sk first dc, dc in next dc, *ch 1, sk next ch-1 space, dc in ea of next 2 dc; rep from * 6 (6, 7, 7) times, turn, leaving rem sts unworked—7 (7, 8, 8) ch-1 spaces.

ROW 2: Ch 3 (counts as dc), V-st in ea ch-1 space across, dc in top of ch-3 turning ch—7 (7, 8, 8) V-sts. Fasten off.

Right Shoulder

ROW 1: With WS facing, sk 11 (14, 15, 18) V-sts to the left of last st made in Row 1 of Left Shoulder, join yarn in next dc, ch 3, *ch 1, sk next ch-1 space, dc in ea of next 2 dc; rep from * across, ending with last dc in turning ch, turn—7 (7, 8, 8) ch-1 spaces.

ROW 2: Ch 3 (counts as dc), V-st in ea ch-1 space across, dc in top of ch-3 turning ch—7 (7, 8, 8) V-sts. Secure last st. Weave in ends.

Left Front

Ch 49 (55, 58, 64).

ROW 1: Ch 4 (counts as dc, ch 1), dc in 5th ch from hook, *sk next 2 ch, V-st in next ch; rep from * across, turn—17 (19, 20, 22) V-sts.

Work same as Back through Row 27 (27, 29, 29).

Shape Armhole

ROW 1 (1ST DEC ROW): Ch 3 (counts as dc, ch 1), sk next ch-1 space, dc in ea of next 2 dc, *ch 1, sk next ch-1 space, dc in ea of next 2 dc; rep from * across to within last 3 ch-1 spaces, sk next ch-1 space, dc in next dc, turn, leaving rem sts unworked—14 (16, 17, 19) ch-1 spaces.

ROW 2 (2ND DEC ROW): Ch 3, sk first 3 dc, dc in next ch-1 space, work V-st in ea ch-1 space across, turn—13 (15, 16, 18) V-sts.

ROW 3 (3RD DEC ROW): Ch 3 (counts as dc, ch 1), sk next ch-1 space, *dc in ea of next 2 dc, ch 1, sk next ch-1 space; rep from * across to within last 3 sts, dc in next dc, sk next dc, dc in top of ch-3 turning ch, turn—13 (15, 16, 18) ch-1 spaces.

Shape Neck

ROW 1 (EVEN): Ch 3 (counts as dc), V-st in ea ch-1 space across working the last rep in the ch-3 sp at the end of the row, turn—13 (15, 16, 18) V-sts.

ROW 2 (EVEN): Ch 3 (counts as dc), sk next ch-1 space, dc in ea of next 2 dc, *ch 1, sk next ch-1 space, dc in ea of next 2 dc; rep from * across, ending with last dc in 3rd ch of turning ch, turn—13 (15, 16, 18) ch-1 spaces.

ROW 3 (V-ST DEC ROW): Ch 3 (counts as dc), V-st in ea of next 11 (13, 14, 16) ch-1 spaces, 2 dc in the next ch-1 sp, dc in top of ch-3 turning ch, turn—11 (13, 14, 16) V-sts, plus ch-3 at begin of row and 3 dc at the end of the row.

ROW 4 (2-DC DEC ROW): Ch 3 (counts as dc), sk first 2 dc, dc in ea of next 2 dc, *ch 1, sk next ch-1 space, dc in ea of next 2 dc; rep from * across ending with last dc top of ch-3 turning ch, turn—11 (13, 14, 16) ch-1 spaces.

Rep Rows 3–4 4 (6, 6, 8) times—7 (7, 8, 8) ch-1 spaces at end of last row, 12 (16, 16, 20) rows.

Work even in patt until Left Front measures same as finished Back to shoulder. Secure last st. Weave in ends.

Right Front

Work same as Left Front through Row 27 (27, 29, 29).

Shape Armhole

ROW 1 (1ST DEC ROW): Sk first dc, sl st in ea of next 6 sts (2 reps and first st of 3rd rep of Row 1 pattern), ch 3 (counts as first dc), sk next ch-1 space, dc in ea of next 2 dc, *ch 1, sk next ch-1 space, dc in ea of next 2 dc; rep from * across, ending with ch 1, sk next ch-1 space, dc in 3rd ch of ch-4 turning ch, turn—14 (16, 17, 19) ch-1 spaces.

ROW 2 (2ND DEC ROW): Ch 4 (counts as dc, ch 1), dc in next ch-1 space, work V-st in ea ch-1 space across to within last ch-1 space, dc in next ch-1 space, sk next 2 dc, dc in top of ch-3 turning ch, turn—13 (15, 16, 18) V-sts.

ROW 3 (3RD DEC ROW): Ch 3, sk first 2 dc, dc in next dc, *ch 1, sk next ch-1 space, dc in ea of next 2 dc; rep from * across to within last ch-1 space, ch 1, sk next ch-1 space, dc in 3rd ch of ch-4 turning ch, turn—13 (15, 16, 18) ch-1 spaces.

Shape Neck

ROW 1 (EVEN): Ch 4 (counts as dc, ch 1), dc in next ch-1 space, V-st in ea ch-1 space across, dc in top of ch-3 turning ch, turn—13 (15, 16, 18) V-sts.

ROW 2 (EVEN): Ch 3 (counts as dc,), dc in next dc, *ch 1, sk next ch-1 space, dc in ea of next 2 dc; rep from * across to within last ch-1 space, ch 1, dc in 3rd ch of turning ch, turn—13 (15, 16, 18) ch-1 spaces.

ROW 3 (V-ST DEC ROW): Ch 3 (counts as dc), sk next ch-1 space, V-st in ea ch-1 space across, dc in top of ch-3 turning ch, turn—11 (13, 14, 16) V-sts, plus ch-3 at begin of row and 3 dc at the end of the row.

ROW 4 (2-DC DEC ROW): Ch 3 (counts as dc), dc in next dc, *ch 1, sk next ch-1 space, dc in ea of next 2 dc; rep across to within last 3 sts, ch 1, sk next ch-1 space, sk next dc, dc top of ch-3 turning ch, turn—11 (13, 14, 16) ch-1 spaces.

Rep Rows 3–4 4 (6, 6, 8) times—7 (7, 8, 8) ch-1 spaces at end of last row, 12 (16, 16, 20) rows.

Work even in patt until Right Front measures same as finished Back to shoulder. Secure last st. Weave in ends.

Button Band

ROW 1: With RS facing, join yarn at top Left Front edge at beg of Row 3 of Neck Shaping, ch 1, sc evenly across Left Front edge, working 2 sc in ea row-end st, turn.

ROWS 2-7: Ch 1, sc in ea st across, turn.

Secure last st. Weave in ends.

Buttonhole Band

ROW 1: With RS facing, join yarn in bottom right-hand corner of Right Front edge, ch 1, sc evenly across to Row 2 of Neck Shaping, working 2 sc in ea row-end st, turn.

ROWS 2-3: Ch 1, sc in ea sc across, turn.

Place a marker ½" (1cm) below the top edge of the band; place another marker 2" (5cm) above the bottom edge, and place 4 more markers evenly spaced between.

ROW 4: Ch 1, *sc in ea sc to next marker, ch 2, sk next 2 sc; rep from * across, sc in ea st to end, turn.

ROW 5: Ch 1, sc in ea st across, working 2 sc in ea ch-2 space, turn.

ROWS 6-7: Rep Row 2. Secure last st. Weave in ends.

Finishing

Sew Fronts to Back at shoulders. Sew buttons to Button Band, opposite buttonholes.

Basic Sweater

This loose-fitting, drop-shoulder sweater is the perfect comfortable sweater for a cold day. It is a relatively easy project to make since there is no armhole shaping or fitting. To design a sweater all your own, change the pattern stitches to any stitches that match the gauge.

The project shown at left was made using Brown Sheep Lamb's Pride Worsted (85% wool/15% mohair, 4oz./113g, 190yd./174m), color M58, Ink Blue.

SKILL LEVEL
Intermediate

FINISHED SIZE
Finished Bust: 38 (40, 42, 44, 46, 48)" [97 (102, 107, 112, 117, 122)cm]
Length: 22 (23, 24, 25, 25, 26)" [56 (58, 61, 64, 64, 66)cm]
Upper Arm Circumference: 18 (19, 19, 20, 20)" [46 (48, 48, 51, 51)cm]
To fit bust sizes: 36 (38, 40, 42, 44, 46)" [91 (97, 102, 107, 112, 117)cm]

YARN
8 (8, 9, 9, 10, 11) (4oz./113g, 190yd./174m) skeins worsted weight yarn

HOOK
U.S. H (5mm) crochet hook

NOTIONS
Tapestry needle

GAUGE
14 sts and 12 rows in pattern = 4" (10cm)

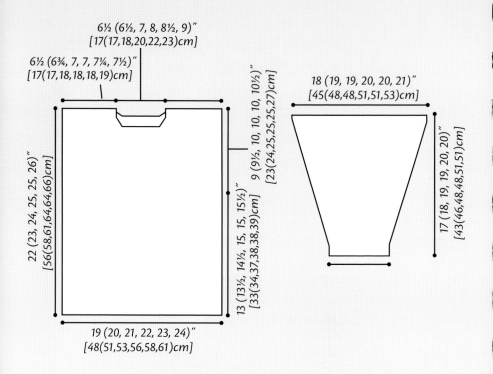

6½ (6½, 7, 8, 8½, 9)"
[17(17,18,20,22,23)cm]

6½ (6¾, 7, 7, 7¼, 7½)"
[17(17,18,18,18,19)cm]

22 (23, 24, 25, 25, 26)"
[56(58,61,64,64,66)cm]

9 (9½, 10, 10, 10, 10½)"
[23(24,25,25,25,27)cm]

13 (13½, 14½, 15, 15, 15½)"
[33(34,37,38,38,39)cm]

19 (20, 21, 22, 23, 24)"
[48(51,53,56,58,61)cm]

18 (19, 19, 20, 20, 21)"
[45(48,48,51,51,53)cm]

17 (18, 19, 19, 20, 20)"
[43(46,48,48,51,51)cm]

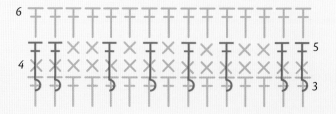

Special Stitches

FPdc: Yo, insert hook from front to back to front again around the post of the next corresponding dc or FPdc 2 rows below, yo, draw yarn through, (yo, draw yarn through 2 loops on hook) twice, sk sc behind FPdc just made.

See Crochet Abbreviations on page 245.

Note: The turning chain at the beg of ea row does not count as a stitch.

Back

Ch 68 (70, 74, 78, 84, 88).

ROW 1 (RS): Ch 3, dc in 4th ch from hook and ea ch across, turn—68 (70, 74, 78, 84, 88) sts.

ROW 2: Ch 1, sc in the front loop only of ea dc across, sk turning ch, turn—68 (70, 74, 78, 84, 88) sts.

ROW 3: Ch 1, starting in first sc, *sc in next sc, dc in next sc; rep from * across, turn—68 (70, 74, 78, 84, 88) sts.

ROW 4: Ch 1, starting in first dc, *sc in next dc, dc in next sc; rep from * across, turn—68 (70, 74, 78, 84, 88) sts.

Rep Row 4 until piece measures 20½ (21½, 22½, 23½, 23½, 24½)" [52 (55, 57, 60, 60, 62)cm] from beginning, ending with a RS row.

Left Shoulder Shaping

ROW 1 (WS): Ch 1, *sc in next dc, dc in next sc; rep from * 10 (11, 11, 11, 12, 12) times, sc in ea of next 2 sts, turn, leaving remaining sts unworked—24 (26, 26, 26, 28, 28) sts.

ROW 2: Ch 2, sk first sc, dc in next sc, *sc in next dc, dc in next sc; rep from * 10 (11, 11, 11, 12, 12) times, turn—23 (25, 25, 25, 27, 27) sts.

ROW 3: Ch 1, *sc in next dc, dc in next sc; rep from * 10 (11, 11, 11, 12, 12) times, sc in next dc, turn—23 (25, 25, 25, 27, 27) sts.

ROW 4: Ch 1, sk first sc, *sc in next dc, dc in next sc; rep from * across, turn—22 (24, 24, 24, 26, 26) sts. Secure last st.

Right Shoulder Shaping

ROW 1: With WS facing, sk 20 (18, 22, 26, 26, 28) sts to the left of last st made in Row 1 of Left Shoulder, join yarn in next dc (24th [26th, 26th, 26th, 28th, 28th] st from the left corner), ch 2, dc in next sc, *sc in next dc, dc in next sc; rep from * 10 (11, 11, 11, 12, 12) times, turn—23 (25, 25, 25, 27, 27) sts.

ROW 2: Ch 1, *sc in next dc, dc in next sc; rep from * 10 (11, 11, 11, 12, 12) times, sc in last dc, turn—23 (25, 25, 25, 27, 27) sts.

ROW 3: Ch 1, sk first sc, *sc in next dc, dc in next sc; rep from * across, turn—22 (24, 24, 24, 26, 26) sts.

ROW 4: Ch 1, *sc in next dc, dc in next sc; rep from * across, turn—22 (24, 24, 24, 26, 26) sts. Secure last st. Weave in ends.

Front

Ch 67 (71, 75, 79, 83, 87), turn.

ROW 1 (RS): Ch 3, dc in 4th ch from hook and ea ch across, turn—67 (71, 75, 79, 83, 87) dc.

ROW 2: Ch 1, sc in the front loop only of ea dc across, sk turning ch, turn—67 (71, 75, 79, 83, 87) sc.

ROW 3: Ch 2, starting in first sc, *dc in next sc, sc in next sc; rep from * 12 (13, 14, 15, 16, 17) times, dc in ea of next 15 sts, **sc in next dc, dc in next sc; rep from ** across, turn—67 (71, 75, 79, 83, 87) sts.

ROW 4: Ch 1, starting in first dc, *sc in next dc, dc in next sc; rep from * 12 (13, 14, 15, 16, 17) times, sc in ea of next 15 dc, **dc in next sc, sc in next dc; rep from ** across, turn.

ROW 5: Ch 2, starting in first sc, *dc in next sc, sc in next sc; rep from * 12 (13, 14, 15, 16, 17) times, FPdc in ea of next 2 dc 2 rows below, sc in ea of next 2 sc, (FPdc in next dc 2 rows below, sc in ea of next 2 sc) 3 times, FPdc in ea of next 2 dc 2 rows below, **sc in next dc, dc in next sc; rep from ** across, turn.

ROW 6: Ch 1, *sc in next dc, dc in next sc; rep from * 12 (13, 14, 15, 16, 17) times, dc in ea of next 15 sts, **dc in next sc, sc in next dc; rep from ** across, turn.

Rep Rows 5-6 until piece measures 10 rows less than finished Back ending with a RS row.

Right Shoulder Shaping

ROW 1 (WS): Ch 1, starting in first dc, *sc in next dc, dc in next sc; rep from * 10 (11, 11, 11, 12, 12) times, sc in ea of next 2 sts, turn, leaving remaining sts unworked—24 (26, 26, 26, 28, 28) sts.

ROW 2: Ch 2, sk first sc, dc in next sc, *sc in next dc, dc in next sc; rep from * across, turn—23 (25, 25, 25, 27, 27) sts.

ROW 3: Ch 1, *sc in next dc, dc in next sc; rep from * 10 (11, 11, 11, 12, 12) times, sc in next dc, turn—23 (25, 25, 25, 27, 27) sts.

ROW 4: Ch 1, sk first sc, *sc in next dc, dc in next sc; rep from * across, turn—22 (24, 24, 24, 26, 26) sts.

ROW 5: Ch 1, *sc in next dc, dc in next sc; rep from * across, turn—22 (24, 24, 24, 26, 26) sts.

Rep Row 5 5 times more. Secure last st.

Left Shoulder Shaping

ROW 1: With WS facing, sk 17 (19, 21, 25, 25, 27) sts to the left of last st made in Row 1 of Left Shoulder, join yarn in next sc (24th [26th, 26th, 26th, 28th, 28th] st from the left corner), ch 2, dc in same sc, *sc in next dc, dc in next sc; rep from * 10 (11, 11, 11, 12, 12) times, turn—24 (26, 26, 26, 28, 28) sts.

ROW 2: Ch 2, starting in first sc, *dc in next sc, sc in next dc; rep from * 10 (11, 11, 11, 12, 12) times, dc in next sc, turn, leaving rem dc unworked—23 (25, 25, 25, 27, 27) sts.

ROW 3: Ch 1, sk first dc, *sc in next dc, dc in next sc; rep from * across, sc in last dc, turn—22 (24, 24, 24, 26, 26) sts.

ROW 4: Ch 2, starting in first sc, *dc in next sc, sc in next dc; rep from * across, turn—22 (24, 24, 24, 26, 26) sts.

Rep Row 4 6 times more. Secure last st. Weave in ends.

Sleeves (make 2)

Ch 32 (36, 36, 36, 36, 38), turn.

ROW 1 (RS): Ch 3, dc in 4th ch from hook and ea ch across, turn—32 (36, 36, 36, 36, 38) dc.

ROW 2: Ch 1, sc in the front loop only of ea dc across, sk turning ch, turn—32 (36, 36, 36, 36, 38) sc.

ROW 3 (EVEN): Ch 1, *sc in next sc, dc in next sc; rep from * across, turn—32 (36, 36, 36, 36, 38) sts.

ROW 4 (INC ROW): Ch 1, *sc in next dc, dc in next sc; rep from * across, sc in top of ch-1 turning ch, turn—33 (37, 37, 37, 37, 39) sts.

ROW 5 (INC ROW): Ch 2, dc in first sc, *sc in next dc, dc in next sc; rep from * across, sc in top of ch-1 turning ch, turn—34 (38, 38, 38, 38, 40) sts.

ROW 6 (EVEN): Ch 2, dc in first sc, *sc in next dc, dc in next sc; rep from * across, sc in last dc, turn— 34 (38, 38, 38, 38, 40) sts.

ROW 7 (INC ROW): Ch 2, dc in first sc, *sc in next dc, dc in next sc; rep from * across, sc next dc, dc in top of ch-2 turning ch, turn—35 (39, 39, 39, 39, 41) sts.

ROW 8 (INC ROW): Ch 1, *sc in next dc, dc in next sc; rep from * across, sc in next dc, dc in top of ch-2 turning ch, turn—36 (40, 40, 40, 40, 42) sts.

ROW 9 (EVEN): Ch 1, *sc in next dc, dc in next sc; rep from * across, turn—36 (40, 40, 40, 40, 42) sts.

Rep Rows 4–9 7 (7, 7, 8, 8, 8) times—64 (68, 68, 72, 72, 74) sts. Work even in patt until sleeve measures 17 (18, 19, 19, 20, 20)" [43 (46, 48, 48, 51, 51)cm]. Secure last st. Weave in ends.

Assembly

Block all pieces. Sew Front to Back across shoulders. Center the Sleeves over the shoulder seam and sew in place. Sew the Front to the Back at the side and under-arm seams.

Neck Trim

RND 1: With RS facing, join yarn in right shoulder seam on neck edge, ch 1, sc evenly around neck opening, sl st in first sc to join.

RND 2: Ch 3, dc in ea sc around, sl st in top of beg ch-3 to join. Secure last st. Weave in ends.

Basic Bead
Crochet Bracelets

These bracelets are easier to make than solid color ropes, since you are always working in the stitch with the same color bead as the bead you are adding, making it easy to know where to put the hook. This color order of beads creates a spiraling, striped pattern. The changing sizes of the beads form the wavy spiral shape of the bracelets.

The project shown at left was made using DMC Size 8 pearl cotton in color #334.

SKILL LEVEL
Intermediate

FINISHED SIZE
Approx. 7½"–8" (19cm-20cm) circumference

YARN
1 (87yd./80m) ball Size 8 pearl cotton

HOOK
U.S. 10 (1.3mm) steel crochet hook

NOTIONS
Beading needle and small length of beading thread
300 size 11 seed beads in 3 colors, 100 beads each
200 size 5 to size 8 seed beads in 2 colors, 100 beads each
100 4mm crystal bicone beads

Special Stitches

Beaded ch (Bch): Slide bead up to hook, yo, draw yarn through loop on hook.

Beaded sl st (Bsl st): Insert hook in next st, slide bead up to hook, yo, draw yarn through st and loop on hook.

See Crochet Abbreviations on page 245.

Stringing the beads

String the beads onto the thread, one bead of each color in the same order for each repeat, until you have all the beads on the yarn. If you are using beads of different sizes, group the small ones together so your bracelet will have an undulating wave. The easiest way to string the beads is to make a line of piles of beads in the order you want to string them, so all you have to do is pick up one bead from each pile down the row, then go back to the beginning and pick up another bead from each pile, repeating until you have all the beads on the thread.

Crocheting the bracelet

Note: You will be working counterclockwise from the inside of the tube.

Make a slip knot about 8" (20cm) from the tail, work 6 Bch, do not join. Work in a spiral throughout.

RND 1: To begin making the spiral, *insert hook into the first Bch you made, holding the bead that is in the Bch behind the hook, slide the next bead up to hook (this bead will be the same color as the bead in the st that the hook is in), yo, draw yarn through st and loop on hook (Bsl st made); rep from * in each st around, do not join, continue to work in a spiral.

Rep Rnd 1 until bracelet measures 7½"-8" (19cm-20cm) long, hold the ends together to see if the bracelet is big enough to fit on your wrist. The bracelet will stretch a little to fit over your hand. When the rope is long enough, end with the 6th bead of the sequence. Cut the thread to about 12" (30cm). Thread with a tapestry needle and sew the ends together being careful to line up the bead colors so the stripes are uninterrupted around the bracelet. Weave in ends.

Granny Square Coaster

Coasters are easy, quick projects that can be made using yarn or thread. They are good small projects to use as gifts or to try out colors and patterns. This simple granny square uses one skein of each color to create a shading of greens and browns.

The project shown at left was made using DMC six-strand embroidery floss in colors: #471 (A), #988 (B), #937 (C), #934 (D), #829 (E), #975 (F) and #783 (G).

SKILL LEVEL
Intermediate

FINISHED SIZE
Approx. 4" (10cm) square

YARN
7 (8¾yd./8m) skeins
six-strand embroidery floss,
1 in each of 7 colors (A, B, C,
D, E, F and G).

HOOK
U.S. E (3.5mm) crochet hook

NOTIONS
Tapestry needle

GAUGE
First 3 rnds = 1¾"
(4cm) square

See Crochet Abbreviations on page 245.

With yarn A, ch 4.

RND 1: (3 dc, ch 2, 4 dc, ch 2, 4 dc, ch 2, 4 dc) in 4th ch from hook, ch 2, sl st in top of beg ch-4 to join—4 ch-2 corner spaces. Fasten off yarn A, join yarn B.

RND 2: With yarn B, ch 5 (counts as dc, ch 2), *(4 dc, ch 2, 4 dc) in next ch-2 space; rep from * 3 times, (4 dc, ch 2, 3 dc) in next ch-2 space, sl st in top of beg ch-3 to join. Fasten off yarn B, join yarn C.

RND 3: With yarn C, ch 3 (counts as dc), 3 dc in ch-2 space, ch 2, *(4 dc, ch 2, 4 dc) in next ch-2 space**, ch 2, 4 dc in next ch-2 space, ch 2; rep from * twice; rep from * to ** once more, ch 2, sl st in top of beg ch-3 to join. Fasten off yarn C, join yarn D.

RND 4: With yarn D, ch 5 (counts as dc, ch 2), 4 dc in next ch-2 space, ch 2, *(4 dc, ch 2, 4 dc) in next ch-2 space**, (ch 2, 4 dc) in each of next 2 ch-2 spaces; rep from * twice; rep from * to ** once more, ch 2, 4 dc in next ch-2 space, ch 2, 3 dc in next ch-2 space, sl st in top of beg ch-3 to join. Fasten off yarn D, join yarn E.

RND 5: With yarn E, ch 3 (counts as dc), 3 dc in next ch-2 space, ch 2, 4 dc in next ch-2 space, ch 2, *(4 dc, ch 2, 4 dc) in next ch-2 space**, (ch 2, 4 dc) in each of next 3 ch-2 spaces, ch 2; rep from * twice; rep from * to ** once more, ch 2, 4 dc in next ch-2 space, ch 2, sl st in top of beg ch-3 to join. Fasten off yarn E, join yarn F.

RND 6: With yarn F, ch 5 (counts as dc, ch 2), (4 dc, ch 2) in each of next 2 ch-2 spaces, *(4 dc, ch 2, 4 dc) in next ch-2 space**, (ch 2, 4 dc) in each of next 4 ch-2 spaces; rep from * twice; rep from * to ** once more, ch 2, 4 dc in next ch-2 space, ch 2, 3 dc in next ch-2 space, sl st in top of beg ch-3 to join. Fasten off yarn F.

RND 7: With RS facing, join yarn G in next ch-2 space, ch 1, sc in first ch-2 space, [(2 dc, ch 3, 2 dc) bet center 2 dc of next 4-dc group, sc in next ch-2 space] twice, *(2 dc, ch 3, 2 dc) bet center 2 dc of next 4-dc group, (sc, ch 3, sc) in next ch-2 corner space **, [(2 dc, ch 3, 2 dc) bet center 2 dc of next 4-dc group, sc in next ch-2 space] 5 times; rep from * twice; rep from * to ** once more, [(2 dc, ch 3, 2 dc) bet center 2 dc of next 4-dc group, sc in next ch-2 space] twice, (2 dc, ch 3, 2 dc) bet center 2 dc of next 4-dc group, sl st in first sc to join. Secure last st. Weave in ends.

Glossary

Afghan hook - A specialized crochet hook used for Tunisian crochet that is as long as a knitting needle, with a hook at one end and a knob at the other.

Back stitch - A decorative embroidery stitch and a firm structural stitch made by working small, adjacent stitches on the front of the piece and long, overlapping stitches on the back. This stitch is often used to outline design elements in embroidery and to attach shoulder seams in garments.

Block - The process of dampening finished crochet work, shaping it to the desired finished size and letting it dry.

Bobble - A raised textural stitch that creates a three-dimensional ball shape on the surface of the fabric; made by working several stitches in the same location then reducing them to one stitch as you complete the stitch.

Cable - A pattern element characterized by one or more stitches that have been worked out of order so that the resulting pattern has a twist in the columns of stitches.

Cluster - A group of stitches worked over one or more stitches, then gathered together into one stitch as the stitch is completed.

CroKnit - also known as double-ended crocheting, Croknit or Crochenit. Worked similar to Tunisian crochet except the work is turned and worked from both ends of a double-ended hook using two balls of yarn.

Dye lot - A unique number or code assigned to skeins of yarn dyed at the same time. When purchasing yarn, choosing skeins from the same dye lot ensures the skeins will all be exactly the same color.

Ease - Stretching or slightly gathering an edge to fit in place. Used mostly when seaming sleeves in place to the front and the back of finished sweaters.

Gauge - The number of stitches and rows per inch on a crocheted project, usually measured over 4" (10cm).

Hank - A wound length of yarn.

Hook gauge - A flat device with different sized holes used to measure the size of a crochet hook.

Mattress stitch - A stitch used to seam finished pieces of crochet together; take a small stitch on one edge of the piece, then take a small stitch on the edge of the other piece and pull the stitches snugly to draw the edges together.

Pattern repeat - A single section of a pattern that is then worked the number of times desired to make the pattern continue over the row of crochet.

Popcorn - A raised texture stitch that creates a three-dimensional ball shape on the surface of the fabric, made by working several stitches in the same location, then reducing them to one stitch as you complete the stitch. A popcorn is generally larger than a bobble.

Post - The vertical section of a crochet stitch.

Ribbing - A knitting pattern traditionally made of knit/purl patterned vertical stripes, used at the waist, cuffs and neck of a sweater, which pulls in more than the rest of the knitting and has more stretch. Crochet has a rib stitch that resembles knitted ribbing, though it doesn't have the same elasticity as a knitted ribbing.

Selvedge stitch - A stitch worked at the edge of a piece in addition to any pattern instructions, used as an added section where the finished pieces will be sewn together.

Shell - A group of stitches worked in the same location creating a fan or shell shape.

Steam blocking - Using a steam iron to dampen finished crochet work before shaping it to the finished size. The iron is held above the piece, never pressed on the surface.

Stitch marker - A small open loop or ring to slide onto the crochet work to mark a pattern detail, such as a place to increase or decrease, or a color or pattern change. When you get to the stitch marker on the row, you work the intended stitch pattern, then move the marker to the stitch just completed, so it is marked for the next row.

Stranding - In colorwork, stranding is when you hold the color not in use to the backside of the work until needed. The result is long and short strands of yarn across each row on the back of the finished piece.

Tapestry needle - A large, blunt-ended needle, with an eye large enough to thread with yarn.

Tunisian crochet - A type of crochet in which all the stitches in each row are worked in two steps. In the first step, the stitches are all picked up onto a long straight hook, called an afghan hook, that resembles a knitting needle with a hook at the end. In the second step, the stitches are worked off the afghan hook, finishing the row.

Yarn weights - Generally, the thickness of yarn. See the chart on page 247 for standard yarn weights.

Crochet Abbreviations

approx - approximately
beg - begin, beginning
Bch - beaded chain
BPdc - back post double crochet
BPsc - back post single crochet
B sl st - beaded slip stitch
ch - chain
ch sp - chain space
cont - continue, continuing
dc - double crochet
dec - decrease
dtr - double triple crochet
ea - each
est - established
foll - follows, following
FPdc - front post double crochet
FPsc - front post single crochet
hdc - half double crochet
hk - hook
htr - half triple crochet
inc - increase

lp(s) - loop, loops
m - marker
MB - make bobble
meas - measure, measures
patt - pattern
pm - place marker
rem - remain, remaining
rep(s) - repeat, repeats
rnd(s) - round, rounds
RS - right side
sc - single crochet
sk - skip
sl - slip
sm - slip marker
sp - space
st(s) - stitch, stitches
tbl - through back loop
tog - together
tr - triple crochet
WS - wrong side
yo - yarn over

Crochet Symbols

- beginning slip knot
- slip stitch
- foundation stitch chain
- chain stitch
- single crochet
- single crochet in reverse direction
- single crochet in a lower row
- slip stitch with a bead
- chain stitch with a bead
- single crochet with a bead
- single crochet in the front half of the stitch
- single crochet in the back half of the stitch
- front post single crochet
- back post single crochet
- half double crochet
- half double crochet in the front half of the stitch
- half double crochet in the back half of the stitch
- double crochet
- double crochet in the front half of the stitch

- double crochet in the back half of the stitch
- front post double crochet
- back post double crochet
- crossed front post double crochet
- front or back post double crochet in row below
- double crochet cluster
- double crochet popcorn
- half double crochet cluster
- double crochet cluster
- half triple crochet
- triple crochet
- double triple crochet

Yarn Weight Guidelines

Since the names given to different weights of yarn can vary widely depending on the country of origin or the yarn manufacturer's preference, The Craft Yarn Council of America has put together a standard yarn weight system. Look for a picture of a skein of yarn with a number 0–6 on most kinds of yarn to figure out its "official" weight. Gauge is given over 4" (10cm) of Stockinette stitch. The information in the chart below is taken from www.yarnstandards.com.

YARN WEIGHT SYMBOL & CATEGORY NAMES	0 LACE	1 SUPER FINE	2 FINE	3 LIGHT	4 MEDIUM	5 BULKY	6 SUPER BULKY
Type of Yarns in Category	Fingering 10-count crochet thread	Sock, Fingering, Baby	Sport, Baby	DK, Light Worsted	Worsted, Afghan, Aran	Chunky, Craft, Rug	Bulky, Roving
Knit Gauge Range* in Stockinette Stitch to 4 inches	33–40** sts	27–32 sts	23–26 sts	21–24 st	16–20 sts	12–15 sts	6–11 sts
Recommended Needle in Metric Size Range	1.5–2.25 mm	2.25—3.25 mm	3.25—3.75 mm	3.75—4.5 mm	4.5—5.5 mm	5.5—8 mm	8 mm and larger
Recommended Needle U.S. Size Range	000–1	1 to 3	3 to 5	5 to 7	7 to 9	9 to 11	11 and larger
Crochet Gauge* Ranges in Single Crochet to 4 inch	32–42 double crochets**	21–32 sts	16–20 sts	12–17 sts	11–14 sts	8–11 sts	5–9 sts
Recommended Hook in Metric Size Range	Steel*** 1.6–1.4 mm	2.25—3.5 mm	3.5—4.5 mm	4.5—5.5 mm	5.5—6.5 mm	6.5—9 mm	9 mm and larger
Recommended Hook U.S. Size Range	Steel*** 6, 7, 8 Regular hook B–1	B–1 to E–4	E–4 to 7	7 to I–9	I–9 to K–10 ½	K–10 ½ to M–13	M–13 and larger

* GUIDELINES ONLY: The above reflect the most commonly used gauges and needle or hook sizes for specific yarn categories.

** Lace weight yarns are usually knitted or crocheted on larger needles and hooks to create lacy, openwork patterns. Accordingly, a gauge range is difficult to determine. Always follow the gauge stated in your pattern.

*** Steel crochet hooks are sized differently from regular hooks—the higher the number, the smaller the hook, which is the reverse of regular hook sizing.

Crochet Hook Conversions

Hooks for Yarn Crochet

diameter (mm)	U.S. size
2.25	B/1
2.75	C/2
3.25	D/3
3.5	E/4
3.75	F/5
4	G/6
5	H/8
5.5	I/9
6	J/10
6.5	K/10½
8	L/11
9	M/13, N/13
10	N/15, P/15
15	P/Q
16	Q
19	S

Hooks for Thread Crochet

diameter (mm)	U.S. size
.75	14
.85	13
1	12
1.1	11
1.3	10
1.4	9
1.5	8
1.65	7
1.8	6
1.9	5
2	4
2.1	3
2.25	2
2.75	1
3.25	0
3.5	00

Metric Conversion Chart

to convert	to	multiply by
Inches	Centimeters	2.54
Centimeters	Inches	0.4
Feet	Centimeters	30.5
Centimeters	Feet	0.03
Yards	Meters	0.9
Meters	Yards	1.1

Resources

Yarn from the following companies was used for the projects in this book. The swatches in Chapter 2, except for the thread crochet sections, were crocheted using Cascade Yarn Cascade 220 (100% wool, 3½oz./100g, 220yd./200m). Look for this and other yarns at your favorite yarn store.

Yarn

Berroco
www.berroco.com

Brown Sheep Company
www.brownsheep.com

Cascade
www.cascadeyarns.com

DMC
www.dmc-usa.com

Knit One Crochet Too
www.knitonecrochettoo.com

Rowan
www.knitrowan.com

Web Sites and Online Magazines

About.com: Crochet
www.crochet.about.com

Crochet Me
www.crochetme.com

beadcrochet dot com
www.beadcrochet.com

Magazines

Interweave Crochet
www.interweavecrochet.com

Crochet World
www.crochet-world.com

Crochet!
www.crochetmagazine.com

Associations

Crochet Guild of America
www.crochet.org

Index

Add More Fiber to Your Life